The Communal Age in Western Europe, c.*1100–1800* offers a fresh interpretation of the significance of towns, villages and parishes in the medieval and early modern period. Drawing on a wide range of primary and secondary sources from numerous regions, Beat Kümin:

- explains how local communities empowered common people through collective agency and a degree of local autonomy
- demonstrates how communal units impacted on key historical developments, from the Reformation to state formation
- provides case studies of the Italian city, the English parish and the village in the Holy Roman Empire
- surveys communal origins, constitutions and cultural representations, as well as contested issues such as gender roles and inner tensions
- evaluates related historiographical debates on communalism and republicanism.

Informed by a genuinely comparative and integrated approach, this original volume offers an excellent introduction to history 'from below', and to the fundamental building blocks of European society.

Beat Kümin is Professor of Early Modern European History at the University of Warwick.

Studies in European History are designed to present the 'state of the debate' on important themes and episodes in European history since the sixteenth century in a clear and critical way for students. Each book carries its own interpretations and conclusions, while locating the discussion firmly in the centre of the current issues as historians see them.

Studies in European History Series

Studies in European History
Series Standing Order ISBN 978–0–333–79365–7
(outside North America only)

You can receive future titles in this series as they are published by placing a standing order. Please contact your bookseller or, in case of difficulty, write to us at the address below with your name and address, the title of the series and the ISBN quoted above.

Customer Services Department, Macmillan Distribution Ltd,
Houndmills, Basingstoke, Hampshire, RG21 6XS, UK

The Communal Age in Western Europe, c.1100–1800

Towns, Villages and Parishes in Pre-Modern Society

Beat Kümin

First published 2013 by
PALGRAVE MACMILLAN

Palgrave Macmillan in the UK is an imprint of Macmillan Publishers Limited, registered in England, company number 785998, of Houndmills, Basingstoke, Hampshire RG21 6XS.

Palgrave Macmillan in the US is a division of St Martin's Press LLC, 175 Fifth Avenue, New York, NY 10010.

Palgrave Macmillan is the global academic imprint of the above companies and has companies and representatives throughout the world.

Palgrave® and Macmillan® are registered trademarks in the United States, the United Kingdom, Europe and other countries.

ISBN 978–0–230–53685–2

This book is printed on paper suitable for recycling and made from fully managed and sustained forest sources. Logging, pulping and manufacturing processes are expected to conform to the environmental regulations of the country of origin.

A catalogue record for this book is available from the British Library.

A catalog record for this book is available from the Library of Congress.

Contents

Contents

List of Figures

Editors' Preface

The Studies in European History series offers a guide to developments in a field of history that has become increasingly specialized with the sheer volume of new research and literature now produced. Each book has three main objectives. The primary purpose is to offer an informed assessment of opinion on a key episode or theme in European history. Secondly, each title presents a distinct interpretation and conclusions from someone who is closely involved with current debates in the field. Thirdly, it provides students and teachers with a succinct introduction to the topic, with the essential information necessary to understand it and the literature being discussed. Equipped with an annotated bibliography and other aids to study, each book provides an ideal starting point from which to explore important events and processes that have shaped Europe's history to the present day.

Books in the series introduce students to historical approaches which in some cases are very new and which, in the normal course of things, would take many years to filter down to textbooks. By presenting history's cutting edge, we hope that the series will demonstrate some of the excitement that historians, like scientists, feel as they work on the frontiers of their subjects. The series also has an important contribution to make in publicizing what historians are doing, and making it accessible to students and scholars in this and related disciplines.

Julian Jackson
Peter H. Wilson

Preface

It was Peter Wilson who first suggested that I write a book on local communities for 'Studies in European History'. I am grateful to him and the other series editors for their encouragement and to the staff at Palgrave Macmillan for all the support and patience during the production process. Special thanks go to my Warwick colleague Humfrey Butters for his help with Chapter 1, and to C. Scott Dixon for commenting on a full draft of this book. The text has also benefitted from the suggestions of two anonymous readers.

The Communal Age is dedicated to my university teachers, especially Patrick Collinson†, who guided my first steps in Anglophone academia. He is sadly missed both within and far beyond the historical community.

BK
Warwick

Notes on the Text

Unless otherwise indicated, quotations from non-English works have been translated into modern English by the author.

The numbers in square brackets refer to the list of primary sources, secondary texts and web materials in the bibliography at the end of the book.

Introduction

This is a book about an empowering force in European history. Lacking privileges conveyed by birthright (like the nobility) or religious authority (like the clergy), the common people acquired social and political influence through association. From the High Middle Ages, out of a variety of causes, Europeans developed local communities in which they organized public affairs with at least partial autonomy and relatively broad participation. These became the chief frameworks for the articulation of interests by burghers and peasants until the rise of general enfranchisement in the modern period. The following chapters offer an introductory survey to the 'Communal Age' in western Europe between the eleventh and eighteenth centuries. In an attempt to overcome common demarcations in the field, the perspective extends over different settings (urban, rural), spheres (secular, ecclesiastical), timeframes (medieval, early modern) and regions (especially English-, German- and Italian-speaking areas).

At the centre of attention, therefore, are the towns, villages and parishes in which people lived. The first two settlement types dominated the secular landscape: villages provided homes and protection for the peasantry, i.e. the vast majority of pre-modern Europeans, while a much smaller number of towns distinguished themselves by a separate legal status and a stronger focus on market exchange. Parishes, the basic units of the ecclesiastical network, cut across this urban/rural divide by providing every man, woman and child with access to the Christian sacraments and a place of worship in the local church. At first sight, therefore, the three types of association appear quite distinct, but – once we turn to underlying structures, collective activities and cultural values – they also had much in common. The ensuing survey attempts to assess these similarities, differences and their wider significance for pre-modern

1

European society. Following remarks on definitions, thematic structure, regional coverage and chronological scope, the remainder of this Introduction summarizes the state of scholarship and the principal research questions underlying the argument.

Definitions, themes and chronological scope

The notion of 'community' continues to fascinate scholars as well as a wider public, particularly at a time when a process of accelerated 'globalization' threatens to efface regional identities and loosen small-scale associations [49; 47; 303]. This is not, however, a book about the concept of 'community' in general. Mindful of legitimate reservations against its proliferation, ambiguity and indiscriminate application (George A. Hillery identified roughly a hundred varieties well over fifty years ago [53]), the focus here lies on bonds of a very specific nature. Terminological definition thus forms an essential first task.

Throughout this study, the phrase 'local communities' will be used as a generic term for small-scale topographical units, in which more or less extensive bodies of (male) members utilized shared resources and institutions to exercise a range of rights and duties on behalf of their fellow inhabitants. The combined features of *locality*, *spatial* circumscription, *horizontal* social organization, (relative) *inclusiveness*, *multifunctionality* and collective *liability* distinguish local communities from other types of association built on *biological* or *cultural* affinities (e.g. families/ethnicities), *personal* power (noble leagues), *vertical* subordination (manors, clientele systems), *spiritually* motivated separation (religious orders, sects), *central* direction (states) and *specific* shared interests (scientific networks, religious fraternities, political parties). 'Local community' is preferred over 'commune' because of the latter's predominantly secular and political connotations. The principal types of towns, villages and parishes, furthermore, will be reassessed in the light of both traditional scholarly priorities – like their constitution and social structure – and more recent 'cultural' approaches – i.e. with sensitivity to their identities, representations, inter-personal relationships, dynamic evolution and often fluid boundaries [238; 278].

Concentration on local communities as defined above does not imply that other types of association were of little importance.

Corporations of various kinds, such as *Alpgenossenschaften* in mountainous areas, or craft guilds in towns, united members with shared socio-economic interests; religious houses provided intercessory and charitable services for the local laity; wards and neighbourhoods served a wide range of administrative and practical purposes; bodies of court jurors and representative assemblies fostered further ties within districts and counties. All of these would have to be taken into consideration for a full assessment of socio-cultural organization, but none acquired quite the same overarching local position as towns, villages and parishes. Neighbourhoods functioned as sub-units of larger urban entities; hundreds and counties represented organs of central government; while socio-economic corporations usually focused on the control of specific resources (like trades, pastures or forests). Yet the boundaries were blurred, and closer investigations into the manifold connections and overlaps remain a task for future research.

Part I of this book provides the empirical foundations through brief overviews of paradigmatic case studies. Focusing on regions where the respective units were particularly strong, we shall look in turn at the 'Italian city', the 'German village' and the 'English parish'. The purpose of these broad overviews is to distil the complexity of actual situations into 'ideal types'. Rather than on exhaustive chronological coverage from 1100 to 1800, the emphasis lies on key themes, such as the emergence, characteristics and transformations of the communal principle. Part II then proceeds to a wider comparative analysis of common features, contextual variables as well as interactions with other local, regional and central bodies. Given the ubiquity of all local communities – there were, of course, parishes on the Italian peninsula, villages in England and numerous towns in the Holy Roman Empire, the results should yield insights for western European society more generally. Eastern parts of the Continent, where feudal powers remained considerably stronger and urbanization relatively less advanced, lie beyond the scope of this inquiry, even though communal structures were certainly not absent there [243; 200]. Part III, finally, focuses on period perceptions, conceptual models and current debates, i.e. the ways in which contemporaries as well as modern observers have engaged with the role of urban, rural and parochial communities in European history.

The chronological scope of this study is large, perhaps over-ambitious. It starts in the High Middle Ages, the time of the first firm evidence for 'local communities' in the narrower sense, and extends over several centuries right up to the Atlantic Revolutions of the late eighteenth century, i.e. the moments when 'equality' and *universal* political rights became fundamental constitutional principles (not always, of course, fully implemented in practice). The latter part of this timespan, from the Renaissance to the Enlightenment, is often linked with the 'rise of the individual', i.e. a period in which confessional division, educational opportunities, growing commercialization and economic self-interest weakened collective bonds, creating tensions within local communities which will need to be addressed in Chapter 4 [237; 242]. It goes without saying that the long-term perspective necessitates a concentration on principal features, prevalent patterns and general change rather than a detailed appreciation of the heterogeneity of situations on the ground. Pre-modern history is rightly characterized as primarily local, and few of this book's findings will be applicable in full for all specific environments, but the main objectives are to lay the foundations, to establish a comparative framework and to propose preliminary conclusions on the nature and significance of the Communal Age in European history. In line with the remit of the 'Studies in European History' series, the argument aims for a balanced discussion of sources, methods and concepts, but also for a fresh interpretation of the phenomenon as a whole. As always, such an account can be neither unbiased nor 'objective'. The author, to lay the cards on the table, leans towards a 'bottom-up' school of historiography, seeing the historical process as shaped, if not driven, by the 'many' rather than the 'few'.

Historiographical approaches

Scholarship in the field is of a bewildering richness and variety. Historiographies of individual regions, types, periods and processes all have a bearing on the study of local communities, not to speak of the various scales – from micro to macro – and national traditions [236]. Again, it would be futile to aim for comprehensive coverage (and indeed even listing) of all relevant contributions. The emphasis has to be on comparative and general works. Naturally, studies in English predominate, but – given the wider geographical scope – many important French, German and Italian

Introduction

titles will also be drawn upon. An annotated list of further reading can be found at the end of the book. The bibliography is divided into primary sources, secondary literature and online materials, each in turn arranged into thematic sections.

So where to start? Two essential points of reference are the works of Otto von Gierke and Ferdinand Tönnies first published in the late nineteenth century. The former studied the long-term development of the phenomenon of association (*Genossenschaft*) as a whole, particularly from a legal and Germanic perspective, covering phenomena as varied as guilds, clubs, sects as well as local communities [50], while Tönnies traced the gradual transformation from a 'natural' society based on custom, personal bonds and shared resources (which he termed *Gemeinschaft*) to one defined by man-made rules, contractual agreements and private property (*Gesellschaft*) [65b]. For much of the twentieth century, where constitutional history loomed large, we find sustained interest in the medieval concept of *universitas*, an umbrella term for different types of association linking people with shared interests, common rules and independent institutions – including bodies as diverse as monasteries, towns and universities [56]. Alongside, students of political thought focused on the 'great minds' and intellectual schools which generated new ideas and ultimately transformed the ways communities, especially in northern Italy and England, were organized [224]. From our perspective, works on guilds (including both secular craft associations as well as religious fraternities), the conciliar movement (which placed the collective power of assembled Church prelates above that of an individual pope), and the development of republicanism are of particular interest [210; 259; 231; 219]. For the latter, concerned with polities in which sovereignty rested in a wider body of citizens rather than a single monarch, scholars usually draw a pretty straight line from classical models – Aristotle's Greek *polis*, where the need for face-to-face exchange among equals limited the size to a few thousand inhabitants [33: iii. 17, vii. 4] – via the constitutional debates of the Italian Renaissance, English seventeenth-century revolutions and the Enlightenment – represented by jurists and philosophers like Bartolus of Sassoferrato, Machiavelli, James Harrington, Montesquieu and Jean-Jacques Rousseau – to the proto-democratic revolutionaries of the Atlantic world [222].

While of unquestionable contextual relevance, the above are probably not the best places to start investigations of local communities as just defined. Neither are many of the older specialized studies, because of the marked broadening of historiographical agendas over the last generation. The closing decades of the twentieth century saw the rise of, first, social and economic approaches and, more recently, the cultural turn. History as an academic discipline now aspires to capture the entire range of past human interactions, i.e. not just facts, deeds and ideas relating to elites, but also the contributions, perceptions and values of humbler groups. Over and beyond the legal, constitutional and intellectual framework of associations, therefore, relevant works – including those of the 'new' political history (which applies a broad cultural approach to the study of government at all levels) – are now expected to address issues like social composition, economic importance, everyday practice, communication structures, gender roles, symbolic representations and spatial constitutions [254]. As yet, many answers remain elusive, not least due to the fragmentary and terse nature of primary sources, but innovative studies like those of Richard C. Trexler (on civic ritual), Katherine French (on late medieval gender roles), and Rudolf Schlögl (on early modern communication systems) provide tasters of what can be achieved [111; 174; 103].

Regional and period-specific surveys of towns, villages and parishes as well as essay collections on the wider concept of community offer the most convenient introductions to date. Léopold Genicot and Jerome Blum examine developments in the pre-modern countryside [132; 121; cf. 123]; Mack Walker, Eberhard Isenmann, Marino Berengo and Christopher Friedrichs discuss towns [114; 86; 69; 81]; a number of anthologies address medieval parishes [183; 190]; Tom Scott and Richard Mackenney offer comparative studies of city states [105; 92]; Alexandra Shepard and Phil Withington survey community studies for early modern England [64], Robert Armstrong and Tadhg hAnnracháin for early modern Ireland [38] and Michael Halvorson and Karen Spierling for Europe as a whole [51]. Charles H. Parker and Jerry H. Bentley adopt a yet wider comparative scale [58], while Anthony Molho, Diogo Ramada Curto and Niki Koniordos focus on related discourses and perceptions [57]. All of these works offer distinctive approaches to key themes such as forms of community, inner structures, conflicting loyalties, patterns of inclusion/exclusion and trends over time.

For theoretical guidance, however, pride of place belongs to Peter Blickle's concept of 'communalism' (discussed in more detail in Chapter 6 [42]), which embeds the constitutional and ideological affinities of German towns and villages into a much wider interpretive framework for pre-modern Europe. Many disciplines in the humanities and social sciences provide additional methodical tools to study networks and hierarchies of communal units [66], while the late twentieth-century 'communitarian' movement attempted to re-balance the weight of individual interests and the needs of wider societies [230]. Closer integration of sociological, anthropological and philosophical perspectives clearly provides a fruitful challenge for future investigations.

Last but not least, numerous sceptical voices have to be taken into account. The concern about terminological imprecision has already been mentioned, but other common charges include the tendency of 'community studies' to romanticize the past by packing it with homogeneous *Gemeinschaften* [267]; to downplay structural tensions within towns, villages and parishes [63]; to ignore the strength of individualist forces [256] and to exaggerate continuities between medieval communes and modern political systems [220]. 'What is common in community', as David Sabean famously stated, 'is not shared values so much as the fact that members of a community are engaged in the same argument' [145: 29–30].

Such reservations need to be taken seriously, but – as the following chapters aim to demonstrate – they do not overturn the historical role and relevance of towns, villages and parishes throughout the areas examined here (and, as an extension of the regional scope to Scandinavia would surely underline, beyond). As long as 'community' is not merely understood as a vague sense of belonging, but a conceptual tool to analyse networks of relationships prompting members to take specific actions, it retains the ability to illuminate 'a very significant part of social life' in pre-modern Europe [45: 127]. It is hoped that the ensuing argument will substantiate this point.

PART I Case studies

The three 'classic' types of local communities in pre-industrial Europe were towns, villages and parishes. Part I examines each of them in regional contexts where they achieved particular prominence. We start with the earliest and most spectacular example of all – a setting where local communities reached the highest degree of autonomy and defined an entire historical era. Their story begins around the first millennium.

1 The Italian City

After a temporary decline of urban life following the collapse of the Roman Empire, the resurgence of trade prompted a new wave of town foundations in the High Middle Ages, from Russia and Scandinavia right across to the Mediterranean. The most extensive 'urban belt' stretched from the Netherlands via the western part of the Holy Roman Empire to the Apennines. At its southern tip, the communes of northern and central Italy became so strong that they 'have no equals ... in other European countries. These cities ..., which were practically independent of the Empire, evolved into genuine city states.' [74: 153]

Towns differed from the surrounding countryside in a number of respects. Common defining features include higher population density, more intensive commercial exchange, distinct legal status, physical demarcation by means of a wall, and greater economic differentiation. The basic unit of organization was the 'house', not just in the sense of a distinct edifice, but of a socio-economic entity – often referred to by the Greek term *oikos* – headed by a householder and encompassing family members as well as apprentices and servants. Houses were embedded in neighbourhoods, often coterminous with parishes, which carried out minor administrative duties like street-cleaning and the supervision of beggars. Known by the Latin term *vicinia*, many had their own assemblies, officers, craft guilds, patron saints and military structures, all of which nurtured strong loyalties as well as rivalries with other quarters [301: 67]. The prosperity of Italian towns rested as much on intense exchange with the surrounding countryside – through bulk trade and large-scale immigration – as on international commerce and monetary transactions. But it is true to say that, for the first time in European history, the 'commercial revolution' of the twelfth and thirteenth centuries created conditions resembling early forms of capitalism: profit orientation, division of labour, signs of factory organization and a nascent financial infrastructure can all be traced in this region, although without eroding the predominance of the aristocracy [87: 185, 325; 91].

Urban society and the birth of the commune

In terms of wealth and status, Italian cities consisted of at least three social layers: the *grandi* – made up of higher nobles, rentiers and clergy – at the top; the *mediocres* – knights, notaries and merchants – in the middle; and the *populus* – smaller traders and labourers – at the bottom of the hierarchy [88]. Any stable regime depended on their coexistence and collaboration, but it goes without saying that relations between these heterogeneous interest groups were not always harmonious. Over the last decades, furthermore, our understanding of urban society has been enriched by a greater awareness of gender roles. Renaissance scholars in particular have uncovered numerous ways in which women, officially subordinate to men in all republics, 'mattered' at the crucial intersection of the private and public spheres, be it in terms of marriage negotiations, religious affairs or property administration [75].

Why did towns emerge and rise so early and strongly in the northern Italian context? In what is known as the pre-communal phase, up to the eleventh century, secular counts and ecclesiastical prelates dominated the political landscape. The Holy Roman Emperors stood at the top of the feudal pyramid, but their influence remained intermittent and power was effectively concentrated in local hands. From around 900, the evidence for town-like settlements becomes widespread all around the northern peninsula. We can trace the granting of individual market privileges rather than elaborate foundation charters as in other parts of the Continent; it looks as if the gradual complementation of the agricultural economy with commercial exchange and associated services occurred rather informally. Cathedral cities like Milan formed the main urban centres, ruled over by bishops who exercised delegated imperial jurisdiction alongside their spiritual functions [112].

Some of the first traces of collective action appear in rural or castle settlements, where freeholding elites joined forces to restore peace in times of frequent conflict. Concerns about the preservation of law and order thus provided important drivers, but this, curiously, placed nobles and aristocrats at the cradle of many Italian city states [87: 143–50]. Initially, the sources reveal only occasional collaboration among leading townsmen, as during a revolt in the Lombard metropolis of Milan as early as 891. At Pavia, members of the people (*popolo*) started to encroach on episcopal prerogatives from the tenth century, showing a sporadic capacity to take independent military initiatives and sustain extended periods of warfare, sometimes even influencing the choice of their bishop [106: 18]. Details on decision-making and organization remain hazy, but municipal consciousness could be enhanced by political crises (like the minority of Emperor Henry IV in the 1050s), resentment of foreign influence, military threats, the granting of market rights or, as has been shown particularly clearly for Milan, anticlerical tensions. What becomes apparent is the gradually increasing wish – or perceived necessity – of urban commercial elites to acquire greater influence in times of political instability [93: 18].

The gradual erosion of episcopal control thus resulted from pragmatic reactions to specific challenges and opportunities rather than a programmatic 'blueprint' for an alternative political system. The actual moment of commune creation remains frustratingly elusive. Legal scholars like Gerhard Dilcher equate it with a sworn union of free townsmen (*coniuratio*), sealed by a collective oath to keep the peace and promote the common good [80; cf. 70: 90]. Most city chronicles, histories and collective memories assume that such an act of conscious seizure of power must indeed have taken place, but not a single example can be unambiguously documented [96: 6–7; for a later oath sworn by the citizens of Volterra in 1224 see 5: 53].

What does exist is evidence for established communes, above all in legal and notarial records from the late eleventh century. A first step was the creation of permanent institutions, crucially a small body of annually changing 'consuls', documented in several cities around 1100: at Milan in 1081, Rome 1083, Pavia 1084, Arezzo 1098, Genoa 1099, Bologna 1123 and Florence 1138, with many further examples [93: 14–17]. At Genoa in 1143, to provide just a flavour of the original constitutional language, the new officials swore:

nos consules electi pro Communi laudabimus et operabimus honorem nostri archiepiscopatus et nostre matris Ecclesie et nostre civitatis de mobile et immobile... Nos non minuemus honorem nostre civitatis, neque proficuum nec honorem nostre matris Ecclesie nobis scientibus. Nos non minuemus iusticiam alicuius nostri concivis pro Communi, neque iusticiam Communis pro aliquo nostro concive, sed equaliter eam observabimus et tenebimus, prout melius rationabiliter bona fide esse cognoverimus ... [301: 149–50].

According to the Genoese oath of office, therefore:

> we – the consuls elected by the commune – will recognize and act in conformity with the honour of our archbishopric and our holy mother Church and our city ... We will not willingly diminish the honour of our city ... We will not do wrong against any of our co-citizens for the benefit of the commune, nor against the commune for the advantage of any co-citizen, but will proceed in an equitable manner, as we recognize sincerely and reasonably to be just.

Apparently composed of representatives elected by fellow townsmen when the institution of the consulate first emerged, later replacements then tended to be made through co-option, i.e. existing consuls obtained the right to choose their successors, albeit on the explicit understanding that the officials acted 'in the name of all citizens', as recorded at Asti in 1095 [286: 231].

Membership of a commune typically derived from inheritance, ownership of a house or regular contributions to taxes and military expenses. Civic oaths played a key role in the periodic reaffirmation and outward representation of the cities. Early on, many of the fundamental decisions must have been taken by a full communal assembly (*arengo*, as documented at Cremona in 1118), but this was gradually replaced by one or two representative councils (at Bassano 40 men made up the small and 100 the large council) chosen in a variety of systems, be it through electors, co-option or sometimes even by drawing lots [113: 32].

A second step was the gradual transfer of executive, legislative and judicial powers from the old lords to the communal institutions. This process, which introduced an alternative to the vertical/feudal ordering of medieval society on the one hand and major new political players on the other, could be assisted by urban alliances, military campaigns and imperial grants. Following a conflict over 'usurped' privileges between Frederick Barbarossa and the Lombard cities, for example, the Peace of Constance of 1183 confirmed the latter's right to elect consuls, pass laws, hold court, exercise regal rights (over forests, pastures, rivers, bridges and mills within their boundaries), erect fortifications and form leagues in return for regular payments and a recognition of the Emperor's overlordship [293]. One of the most tangible aspects of communal government was unprecedented regulatory activity, prompted by a positive belief that the common good could be advanced by proactive interventionism. 'Natural' targets included the prices of commodities, the supervision of trade, the generation of revenues and the enhancement of military capacity, but few aspects of public life remained untouched.

The third step was territorial expansion into the surrounding countryside, i.e. the acquisition of a legally dependent *contado* bolstering the cities' standing through extra manpower, improved grain provisions, a safer commercial environment and financial contributions. This process, moved forward by purchase and negotiation as well as conquest, sparked frequent tensions with neighbouring lords and cities, a situation which in turn fostered corporate awareness and the emergence of a communal identity. Subdivided in *pleberie* under city viscounts, the dependent territories continued to exercise lower jurisdiction, but appeal cases were now heard in the respective capitals. Economic conditions changed through greater market penetration, erosion of serfdom and a stream of urban migration by both peasants and nobles (particularly in times of plague). Three members of the seigneurial Manfredi family, for example, swore allegiance to the commune of Modena in 1168:

> I swear that I will be a citizen and resident of Modena ... and that I will possess a house in the city of Modena by the coming feast of St Martin and defend the city within its boundaries against anyone, except the Emperor: and beyond its territory I will defend the people and property of the citizens of Modena, reserving only the loyalty to lords of whom I am (or will be in future) a vassal. I will endeavour to be of use to the commune of Modena in assemblies and councils and will not prevent the inhabitants of my lands paying tributes in money and labour according to the wishes of the consuls of Modena [301: 158].

Similarly at Alba in 1193, while continuing to live in the country, two inhabitants of the *contado* committed themselves to:

> ... be citizens of Alba and subject to its jurisdiction with regard to their entire freehold estate and all they ever had and will possess ... and in

11111

111

11111111111111

The Communal Age in Western Europe, c.1100–1800

consequence let them be citizens and observe the communal customs like other citizens who permanently reside at Alba [286: 60].

These sources underline the complex interplay of feudal and communal elements in Italian city states. Rural lords retained their social prestige and an independent power base in their estates, but they also acknowledged the political rise of urban society and the benefits of amicable relations with this potential competitor. Recent research thus emphasizes the significant contribution of the *contado* to the fortunes of its commune. Land remained a key resource even in this proto-capitalist environment; compared to many northern European regions, Italian cities acquired a very direct, comprehensive and uniform lordship over their territories; but nobles retained an important say in the government of the city-states. 'Historiographically, the *contado* has conquered the city' [77: 388].

Proliferation and perceptions of communes

The rise of Italy's communes is not just a scholarly concept, but a phenomenon recognized by contemporary observers. Bishop Otto of Freising (d. 1158), an uncle of Emperor Frederick, was startled by the unusual socio-political profile of this region. Shortly before his death, he wrote of the 'Lombards':

> In the governing of their cities ... and in the conduct of public affairs, they still imitate the wisdom of the ancient Romans. ... [T]hey are so desirous of liberty that ... they are governed by the will of consuls rather than rulers. There are known to be three orders among them: captains [great nobles], vavasors [lower feudal vassals], and commoners. And in order to suppress arrogance, the aforesaid consuls are chosen not from one but from each of the classes. And lest they should exceed bounds by lust for power, they are changed almost every year. The consequence is that, as practically that entire land is divided among the cities, ... scarcely any noble or great man can be found in all the surrounding territory who does not acknowledge the authority of his city. And from this power to force all elements together they are wont to call the several lands of each [noble, or magnate] their contado (*comitatus*). Also, that they may not lack the means of subduing their neighbors, they do not disdain to give the girdle of knighthood or the grades of distinction to young men of inferior station and even

16

some workers of the vile mechanical arts, whom other peoples bar like the pest from the more respected and honorable pursuits. From this it has resulted that they far surpass all other states of the world in riches and in power. They are aided in this not only, as has been said, by their characteristic industry, but also by the absence of their princes [i.e. Emperors], who are accustomed to remain on the far side of the Alps. In this, however, forgetful of their ancient nobility, they retain traces of their barbaric imperfection, because while boasting that they live in accordance with law, they are not obedient to the laws. For they scarcely if ever respect the prince to whom they should display the voluntary deference of obedience or willingly perform that which they have sworn by the integrity of their laws, unless they sense his authority in the power of his great army [3: book III, ch. XII, 127–8].

As a prelate steeped in the medieval worldview of social hierarchy and subordination, what startled the bishop most was the integration of nobles into a body of commoners, the elevation of humble people to higher rank and the apparent prosperity of these inauspicious political constructs (due in no small part, he thinks, to the Emperor's frequent absence and failure to suppress them).

Overall, some 200–300 city states (including those technically known as *terre* [towns], *borghi* [burghs] and *castelli* [fortified settlements]) had emerged between the Alps in the north and Naples in the south by the late twelfth century. Most counted between 5,000 and 20,000 inhabitants, and fewer than two dozen acquired full autonomy and dependent territories (*contadi*) of over 1000 km², with Milan, Venice and Florence (whose population doubled from 50,000 to 100,000 over the course of the thirteenth century) representing the extreme examples [113: xvi, 21]. Their mutual relations spanned the entire range from ad-hoc exchange and formal alliances to intense rivalry and military hostilities, with some smaller communes coming to depend on the larger cities. The truly exceptional feature, to re-emphasize the point, was the broadening of political participation and the emergence of a fundamental alternative to the prevailing system of feudal inequality, noble privilege and monarchical government.

In a prolonged, cumulative process of experiment and reform, culminating in the mid- and later thirteenth century, the communes elaborated a system ... designed to secure the fullest or the fittest participation and representation of ... the whole civic community, *communitas civium*. Full participant citizenship to be sure was subject increasingly ... to restriction and regulation. But equally with expansion the citizen body was also vastly increased, and on a scale ... that resulted at its peak in a more extended franchise, broader democratic base, and wider range of participation, political action, and education than in any known regime before the French Revolution. ... Foundation of the system was election, the contrary of hierarchy: popularly based election and general eligibility to offices and functions without regard to status, rank, or presumptive rights to rule, according to divisions not of class but of place, the cross-sectional groupings of neighbourhood, quarter, or local commune [87: 403].

Power and participation

Cities were heterogeneous bodies and their political processes fraught with tensions. Almost from the beginnings in the eleventh century, communes faced the problem of factions. One key issue was the extent of noble power, which manifested itself in a disproportionate share of offices, large groups of vassals and architectural representation. The towers of leading families, erected for protection as well as social prestige, vied with cathedrals and churches for domination of the cityscape. Aristocrats entered into institutionalized associations (*consorterie*) with potentially destabilizing effects on the commune as a whole, as in late twelfth-century Florence [5: 86]. By the mid-1200s, a rival power base had emerged in the shape of the *popolo*, not so much the 'people' as such than middling craftsmen and merchants joining forces to enhance their own influence. Rooted in guilds and neighbourhoods and guided by a 'captain' presiding over a group of elders (*anziani*), the *popolo* acquired a mass following and evolved into a 'state within the state', 'a situation which anyone accustomed to clear-cut modern notions of sovereignty must see as a paradox and nightmare' [113: 139]. During the 1250s, Florence's *popolo* – organized in twenty companies based on the city's militia structure – snatched power from the nobles, as part of a wider trend which mirrored the transfer of authority from the bishops to the communes just over a century before. The chronicler Dino Compagni, an active participant, describes a successive phase (1280–82) in this protracted political struggle as follows:

> When the city faced new dangers by reason of civic discord, some *popolani*, among them Dino [i.e. the author himself], held council: ... and

the frank words of the citizens who spoke of their liberty and the injustices suffered heated them to such a fever pitch ... that they passed orders and laws which would be hard to remove. ... In effect, these laws laid down that they should protect the properties of the commune, to make the noble governors act equitably and to ensure that the small and weak [townspeople] should not be oppressed by the great and powerful. And had these procedures been observed, it would have been to the great utility of the people [2: 35–7].

The overall impact of the movement has been assessed in contrasting terms: while criticized by some historians for its anti-noble agenda and by others for the exclusion of the lower classes, the widening of political participation and the firm support of commercial interests 'had incalculably beneficial effects upon the economy'. In the more abstract sphere of political thought, too, the ascendancy of the *popolo* reverberates in notions of local, more broadly based sovereignty advanced by jurists like Bartolus of Sassoferrato [93: 81–3]. Yet in the longer term, inner divisions – accentuated by the wider tensions between laity and clergy as well as pro-papal Guelfs and pro-imperial Ghibellines in Italian politics – contributed to the decline of the *popolo*.

The unexpected, if ingenious response to the growing urge for concord was the appointment of *podestà*, paid governors imported from other cities for periods of six months at a time. As neutral figureheads, required to uphold local laws and undergo an audit at the end of their term, they represented the commune to the outside world, presided over municipal courts and mediated between different interest groups. By the thirteenth century, legally trained *podestà* moved from town to town and sometimes returned to the same place (one Guglielmo Pusterla from Milan served a number of communes on no fewer than 17 occasions). Another indication of the professionalization of government is the growth of salaried personnel: Pistoia employed 14 in 1200, but 82 in 1300, not to speak of an increasing number of unpaid officials. Out of a population of 5,000, no fewer than 860 men held some sort of civic post at Siena in 1257 – vividly confirming the cities' remarkable level of civic participation [113: 66]. A concurrent expansion in writing produced new types of documents and a need for better record-management. The uniquely rich thirteenth-century archives of Treviso, for example, include statutes, land transfers, jurisdictional privileges, records of debts, feudal inquisitions, notarial transactions, depositions in property disputes, leases of communal tenements, diplomatic correspondence and fiscal registers. Subsequent *podestà* distinguished themselves through a series of administrative reforms, most notably the establishment of a communal chancellery in the 1280s [6: vi, xl and *passim*].

City culture

Public life focused on the workshops, markets, streets, *piazze*, civic buildings, schools and associated leisure facilities – taverns, baths, gambling houses, brothels – of the urban landscape. Churches, ecclesiastical institutions and pious observances played key parts in the forging of communal identities [299]. Recent research on Venice, Florence and other cities has highlighted the role of ceremonies and processions in the creation of political space and the display of the (ever-changing) topography of power. The ritual year consisted of an almost constant sequence of private, corporate and communal events, often involving both religious and secular components. Carnival, with its temporary suspension of constraints on consumption, appearance and behaviour before the austere season of Lent, is the most spectacular and universal example, but each commune had an idiosyncratic calendar which incorporated elements like foundation myths, patronal feast days, neighbourhood competitions and celebrations of military achievements. From the thirteenth century, for example, Venice's maritime identity found expression in the Doge's annual 'marriage of the sea', a rite combining ecclesiastical and sexual imagery to symbolize the city's imperial claims over the eastern Mediterranean [95: part III].

The cultural significance of Italy's communal age can hardly be overstated. Vibrant urban societies with disproportionate economic powers, high educational standards, multiple ecclesiastical institutions and – as new political constructs – enhanced representational needs presented scholars, artists and patrons with an ideal framework for their activities. It is no coincidence that Europe's first university was founded at Bologna in the late eleventh century. Perhaps the most tangible, flexible and enduring cultural manifestation of communal identity, however, is civic architecture in general and the proliferation of town halls in particular. One of the oldest surviving examples – featuring the characteristic multi-storey rectangular

Figure 1 The imposing Palazzo del Popolo (literally 'People's Palace', also known as Palazzo del Bargello) in Florence, dating back to the mid-thirteenth century. Photo: Beat Kümin.

structure with soaring belltower from the early 1200s – stands at Volterra. The succeeding decades saw a game of one-upmanship in municipal palace construction between Siena and Florence. In the latter, the *Palazzo del Popolo* (begun in 1255 as a residence for the captain and later the *podestà*; see Figure 1) survives alongside the *Palazzo Vecchio* (where communal operations were transferred to later on [302]). Previously, in a further illustration of the interweaving of sacred and secular space, civic assemblies had been held in suitably large churches such as the *Duomo* at Florence and San Sisto at Pisa. Town halls then provided prime locations for the artistic celebration of communal values and achievements, most famously expressed perhaps in Ambrogio Lorenzetti's frescos on the effects of good government in the *Palazzo Pubblico* at Siena (1338–9 [107: 39–117]).

Renaissance and early modern developments

By around 1300, Italy's communal age had passed its prime. There is no room here to trace the cities' evolution through to the end of the *ancien régime*, but inner divisions and factional conflict eroded trust in the system of broad political participation from the late thirteenth century. 'As hungry men dream of food and frozen men of warmth, so the men of the Italian republics dreamed of concord'. Sooner or later, rule by a powerful individual gained in attraction for most communities, leading to effective re-feudalization and the takeover of power by military *condottieri* (e.g. Castruccio Castracani at Lucca in the 1320s) and princely dynasties (like the Visconti in Milan from the 1330s). At Ferrara, as early as 1264, Obizzo of Este received a grant of inheritable lordship 'by the wish, consent and order of the whole commune' [113: 156, 169]. Smaller towns tended to be integrated into the dominions of larger entities, yet Italy remained a patchwork of medium-sized urban and princely territories with a wide range of government styles [93: 176–88; 90]. Reflecting on longer-term implications, Jacob Burckhardt famously saw the combination of multiple regimes, political tensions and social fluidity as a springboard for the evolution of secular and rational principles, which – combined with the revival of classical values in the Renaissance – paved the way for the 'conquest of the Western world' [237: 104]. Italy's road to modern democracy was thus anything but linear and straightforward, involving a variety of feudal, aristocratic, monarchical and despotic experiments along the way.

Municipal government did not simply give way to total princely or state control, so a basic foundation of communal structures survived. Yet centuries of domestic power struggles and foreign interference dismantled the once dense network of sovereign localities. The Italian Wars, prompted by a French invasion in 1494, brought a particularly extensive period of disruption, ever-changing alliances and subordination to external priorities. There were some exceptions to the general trend, of course. Florence formally remained a republic until the creation of an inheritable monarchy in the 1530s, Genoa and Venice right up to the Napoleonic Age. Yet constraints appear even in these contexts: the Medici dynasty gained increasing control over the Tuscan metropolis from the fifteenth century, Genoa came under successive Milanese, Spanish and finally French influence, while the constitution of Venice had always been 'mixed' rather than genuinely 'popular', restricting real power to a tiny minority of aristocratic families, an exclusive senate and the quasi-princely figurehead of the Doge.

Summary

The Italian city represents the earliest and most spectacular flourishing of the communal principle. Emerging out of pragmatic responses to local needs, it brought a remarkable widening of political participation, collective resources, extensive urban self-government and a real alternative to the predominant forms of vertical subordination. Following rapid proliferation and territorial expansion in the eleventh and twelfth centuries, the system of the *comune* was gradually undermined by factional strife, oligarchization and the protracted struggle for supremacy over the Italian peninsula. 'Locating communities' thus becomes a yet more ambivalent and complex exercise from the Renaissance period, even though the remarkable story of the old city states would always be remembered by succeeding generations and frequently invoked in their literary and political discourses [74: 164–5; 97; cf. now 105].

From a wider European perspective, the peninsula's prosperity and strategic significance also decreased in line with the shift of economic gravity away from the Mediterranean world to the Atlantic seaboard in the course of the early modern period. New commercial and financial centres emerged north of the Alps, first in the Holy Roman Empire and later the colonial powers of the Dutch Republic and England, while substantial parts of Italy underwent a process of re-feudalization. A study of pre-modern communal culture thus has to extend to other regional contexts as well.

2 The Village in the Holy Roman Empire

Many Imperial Free Cities acquired considerable autonomy, economic clout and territories over the course of the Middle Ages. Nuremberg and Augsburg, in particular, evolved into major European centres, but – compared to the Italian situation just studied above – imperial control remained stronger and the standing of city states weaker north of the Alps [84; 86; 98]. This regional case study thus focuses on another type of local community.

Origins and early evolution

Villages emerged around the first millennium, evolved into corporate bodies of householders with executive, legislative and jurisdictional powers from at least the twelfth century and remained the basic unit of rural organization right until modern times [154: 37 and *passim*]. The precise roots of their formation are contested and may well have varied in different regions. Special conditions, for example, applied in the colonization areas east of the river Elbe, where successive waves of settlement between the ninth and thirteenth century involved a mixture of woodland clearing and expulsion of native Slavonic inhabitants, resulting in (initially at least) advantageous terms for peasant communities [229: Ch. 5]. Three principal explanatory models have been advanced for the western part of the Empire. The first sees clear lines of continuity between groups of vassals *personally* subjected to specific courts and those of later *territorially* defined villages; the second prioritizes feudal/seigneurial factors in the generation of rural communities; and the third emphasizes socio-economic transformations, especially trends towards denser forms of settlement and the erosion of demesne agriculture (*Villikation*) from the thirteenth century. The last process prompted the creation of distinct holdings – where peasants organized their own labour and kept any surpluses – and the ensuing need for practical co-ordination among the tenants of a given locality [119: 29–36]. The fundamental tension affecting villages – as indeed towns and parishes – emerges in all scenarios, namely the delicate balancing of external pressures, individual interests and communal priorities.

It is helpful to form an impression of the sheer numerical significance of the phenomenon. By the close of the Middle Ages, the Holy Roman Empire may have counted some 3,000 towns and 30,000 seigneurial residences, but no fewer than 100,000 villages. In the south-western Duchy of Württemberg alone, over three-quarters of the population lived in 1,200 villages, whose average size fluctuated between 500 inhabitants (in 1490), 1,000 (1560), 400 (following heavy war-related losses in the early 1600s), 1,000 (1720) and 2,000 (in 1800) [281: 96]. The nucleated settlement most commonly associated with the German term *Dorf* – surrounded by gardens, a fence, open fields with crop rotation and common lands of pastures and woods – was only one of several types of rural communities. Others consisted of scattered farmsteads, a series of small hamlets or entire court districts and valleys (as in the central Alps). The legal framework was frightfully complex, with rights over persons, estates, churches and jurisdiction frequently in several hands. Apart from nobles and the Emperor himself, lordship could be exercised by ecclesiastical bodies (bishoprics, religious houses), cities and – with the growing monetarization and commercialization of the economy – individual town burghers [118].

Rural society used to be imagined as homogeneous, static and 'superstitious', but such stereotypes have long been discredited. In each village, householders with extensive holdings lived alongside those with little land and cottagers who relied solely on their labour. Economic inequalities became particularly striking in times of bad harvest or high population pressure, when poorer neighbours had to rely on credit and more or less formal relief, both of which created personal dependencies and intra-communal tensions. Depending on factors like urbanization and terms of tenure, countryfolk could be embedded in local and regional market networks, selling surpluses over subsistence requirements in nearby towns and/or – in proto-industrial regions like Upper Germany and the Netherlands from around 1500 – earning extra income from domestic textile production. Countless places also contained mills, inns, bath-houses and artisanal workshops. Looking at the empire as a whole, at least three main economic landscapes can be distinguished: first and foremost, a predominant agricultural sector (encompassing areas with arable as well as mixed husbandry); second, regions focusing on viticulture (esp. along the rivers Rhine and Mosel) or commercial crops (like flax and wool); and, third, pockets of rural industry (including the large silver mines of the Tyrol) [272: Ch. 4]. Simplifying dramatically, living conditions were relatively favourable at the close of the Middle Ages – when landlords, affected by the 'agrarian crisis' following the Black Death, had to offer tenants comparatively good terms; but increasingly harsh from the sixteenth century – when demographic growth placed great strain on rural society, which then tended to marginalize the landless and close itself off to outsiders. Yet even during these difficult times, the tenants of a Benedictine Abbey in Swabia managed to achieve sizable grain surpluses by means of extensive recourse to local credit and land markets [150]. A considerable amount of the peasantry's spare resources helped to satisfy spiritual needs, not so much in terms of pagan cults and magical activities, but active engagement with mainstream Christian practices like mass foundations, church embellishment, pilgrimages and pious bequests – a wider European phenomenon to be investigated in more detail in Chapter 3.

The late medieval 'golden age' brought substantial improvements in the personal status of many peasants, with serfdom – typically characterized by restrictions on mobility, choice of marriage partners and inheritance rights – eroded by a combination of demographic decline, seigneurial impecunity and acts of resistance. Free peasants remained the exception, but countrydwellers seized any chances to improve their legal position, sometimes with considerable – individual or communal – financial investment. In the Alpine valley of Saanen in 1312, to cite a striking example, the tenants collectively paid for the discontinuation of a tax which symbolized their servile status and subsequently acted as a corporate *communitas* to enhance their position through the purchase of customs rights (1341), redemption of a string of feudal obligations (1371), abolition of death duties (1397) and eventually the termination of all remaining seigneurial privileges (1448, at the exorbitant cost of £24,733). By the fifteenth century, the 'land' of Saanen also possessed a seal as an outward sign of its newly-established autonomy [119: 41–2].

For the traditional feudal elites, the emergence of village communities presented fresh challenges, all the more so as it coincided with parallel developments in towns. The later Middle Ages were difficult enough for smaller nobles and imperial knights. On top of declining agrarian income, they faced early pressures of state formation; the military shift from mounted knights to common infantrymen; the outlawing of private feuding at the Diet of Worms in 1495 and the rise of university-trained bureaucrats in territorial and imperial administration. Many adapted to the new environment by opting to serve the princes, but others saw their family fortunes decrease [283]. From a regional perspective, historians traditionally regarded the river Elbe as the demarcation line between a 'freer' western part of the Empire, where manorial lords demanded only a limited range of dues and services from their tenants, and a 'servile' eastern part, where demesne-based agriculture tied servile peasants to the land. The reality, as we now know, is much more complex. 'Second serfdom' – a seigneurial attempt to reclaim lost power and revenue at the close of the Middle Ages – also affected many areas in the German south-west, while tenurial arrangements varied considerably in the east. A further key variable was market exposure, which in turn depended on location, proximity to major urban centres (of which there were fewer in the east) and the state of the transport infrastructure (also relatively less developed than in the west). Overall, though, there can be no doubt that landlord power over the rural population grew substantially in the course of the early modern period. In a reversal of the late medieval situation, demographic expansion and rising food prices put feudal elites back in the driving seat [158: 112; 272: Ch. 6].

Village culture

As in premodern Europe more generally, hierarchy and patriarchy were basic social principles in German villages. We know much less about the public life of rural women than men, not least due to gender biases inherent in period sources, where 'common man' stands for the politically active householder and 'common woman' for a prostitute [266]. Yet this imbalance is being addressed. A recent study of female contributions to the Württemberg economy, for example, found a very high proportion of extra-domestic activities, but also evidence of attempts by – male-dominated – community institutions to stifle female productivity, consumption and competition [260]. We have also been alerted to the high significance of gendered codes of honour: virility, honesty and the ability to provide for dependants for men; sexual purity and modesty for women. In Lutheran areas, the post-Reformation period offered both opportunities for female advancement – especially an acknowledgement of spiritual equality under a system where salvation derived from 'faith alone' and greater pastoral emphasis on a genuine partnership between husband and wife – as well as setbacks – such as the loss of nunneries and the effective strengthening of the *Hausvater's* control over all members of a household [280: 34–5, 186–95]. As for rural minorities, Jews are probably the best-known example. Following repeated waves of prosecution and expulsions in late medieval towns, many moved to the countryside, if not much further east into Poland-Lithuania. Here, they lived a precarious existence as petty traders, money-lenders and medical practitioners, dependent on the opportunistic protection of territorial princes or imperial knights and excluded from the mainstream institutions of Christian society. Village communities have been branded as anti-Jewish as well as heavily stratified [130], but that was hardly an unusual feature of social organisms at the time. Recent research on the southern German county of Burgau actually reveals a surprising amount of personal contact, business interaction and even conviviality alongside tensions and conflict. Stark generalizations like 'division' or 'integration' cannot do justice to the complexities of the relationship on the ground [277].

In everyday life, conditions were challenging. Limited productivity, elementary technology and dependency on the harvest caused real hardship and periodic subsistence crises. Educational provision was at best rudimentary, and illiteracy the norm well into the modern period. Yet rural life should not be envisaged as bleak and unrewarding. The local topography, history and landmarks fostered a sense of identity and even pride, manifesting itself in fierce rivalry with other villages and costly endeavours to embellish public buildings. 'Sharing space in the village led to shared experiences that fostered a sense of belonging together. Probably no man-made sound was more common in the village than the chiming of the church bell' [152: 50–52]. While bells were rung for special occasions, regular exchange took place outside the houses, on the green, around the church, at fountains, in spinning bees and, above all, in the countless inns, wine taverns and beer houses which provided a wide range of socio-cultural services. Alcohol lubricated all forms of social interaction in pre-modern Europe, including the sealing of business contracts which had to be publicized through a shared drink (*Weinkauf*), and drinking establishments often doubled up as political centres, providing venues for village assemblies, court sessions, electioneering and local government transactions. Thanks to their extensive contacts, financial resources and social capital, innkeepers played a leading part in public affairs, be it as members of councils or as ringleaders of popular resistance [252]. The late medieval calendar, further-more, was rich in religious, secular and family celebrations, often involving sociability, dancing and copious consumption of food and drink. On church dedication day (*Kermis*), villagers organized games, plays and musical entertainment which attracted visitors from far afield. As with carnival, exuberant sociability could spill over into disorder and violence, but informal social control – based on widely shared values like peace and the common good – helped to keep these in check. As always, it is important not to romanticize communal relations. From a modern perspective, the intrusiveness of neighbourly supervision and the emphasis on compliance with customary norms appears stifling. Where the latter were violated, for instance by an older woman marrying a young man, or a wife dominating her husband, shaming rituals like charivari pressu-rized 'offenders' to conform [145; 152: 55; 270].

Village culture rested on face-to-face interaction, but writing complemented it from an early stage. Invaluable evidence derives from collections of customary law (*Weistümer, Offnungen, Taidinge*), as 'revealed' by the most senior and distinguished members of local communities on specific occasions [13; 14]. These cover a wide range of issues and relationships, ranging from inheritance systems and marriage laws via ordinances for local institutions to the rights and obligations of both villagers and lords (demon-strating, as everything else, highly regionalized patterns). Once interpreted as 'pure' repositories of ancient Germanic tradition, more recent research detects a fair amount of seigneurial influ-ence, reflections of specific historical contexts and an element of 'invented tradition' [151]. Evidence for communal rights was carefully stored, periodically confirmed and passed on from generation to generation. Each item formed part of collective memory and could be retrieved centuries after its formulation.

The remarkable micro-republic of Gersau on Lake Lucerne, which governed itself from 1390 – when the villagers (acting through their parochial organization) paid off their feudal lord – to the French invasion of Switzerland in 1798, built up a particularly impressive collection (cf. Figures 2, 6 and Chapter 4 below). The surviving spectrum includes treaties with Swiss cantons, ecclesiastical privileges – including one authorizing the parishioners to appoint their own priest in 1483 – and even an imperial charter of 1433, in which Sigismund effectively placed Gersau under his and all successive Holy Roman Emperors' immediate protection. Many of these documents, such as two early law codes of 1436, carry the community's own seal with a depiction of the patron saint of St Marcellus and the legend 'S[igillum] Comunitatis in Gersow' [12: Charters no. 6, 3, 12, 8, 9–10]. When the villagers decided to pass on information to posterity in a series of chronicles compiled on the occasion of major church repairs from the mid-seventeenth century (all stored in a golden capsule mounted on the church tower), they proudly referred to the 'God-given liberties, obtained by our ancestors from the old Emperors and kings' and preserved in the communal archive [30: 168]. Here as elsewhere, rural life is mirrored in a wide range of sources including council / assembly protocols, accounts, estate surveys, court records, official correspondence, by-laws and tax registers, conveniently accessible – for Switzerland – through a model edition of the entire body of legal documents preserved in regional archives [37], and – for France – an online collection of village records [296].

Political life

Gersau reached an extreme extent of self-government, but the corporate empowerment of village communities was a more general political development over the late medieval centuries:

> The comparatively complicated new rotation system [used to produce more crops at a time of population pressure before the Black

Figure 2 The rural micro-republic of Gersau on Lake Lucerne, arguably Europe's most autonomous village community. This extract from a seventeenth-century prospect of the neighbouring Swiss canton of Schwyz highlights the prominent village hall and parish church (on the left), the gallows representing the community's rights of high jurisdiction (situated centre-left on the shore in the foreground) and the pilgrimage chapel of Maria Hilf (centre-right; no. 9). Matthäus Merian (ed.), *Topographia Helvetiae, Rhaetiae et Valesiae* [1654] (Reprint, from Basel: R. Geering, 1926), between pp. 38–9. Reproduced by kind permission of the Schweizerische Nationalbibliothek NB, Bern.

Death] ruled out individual choices of crops and demanded a process of collective decision-making involving all peasants. To settle the inevitable disputes, some form of local conflict resolution had to be found, while rules and regulations were needed to keep the peace among neighbors who now lived in much closer proximity. The result was the emergence of village autonomy, village jurisdiction, and village legislation as autogeneous rights of the inhabitants[, ...] giving the village – in a manner of speaking – the right to exercise 'state functions'. [40: 3]

Late medieval customary law from present-day Switzerland exemplifies the ubiquity and range of political participation, wherever possible based on the principle of majority decisions:

[Höngg near Zurich, 1338] ... let it be known that each year on St Stephen's day, the headman [*meiger*] and tenants [*hu(o)ber*] of Höngg shall choose and elect a forester, and he who is chosen by the greater part and accepted by the headman, shall be forester ...

[Wülflingen near Winterthur, 1484] ... in whatever the village has to decide, the smaller part shall follow the greater part, without contradiction ...

[Burgau in the Toggenburg, 1469] ... when the bailiff [*vogt*] wants to name an official for his district, it shall be done with the knowledge and will of its inhabitants. Should none be agreed upon, they can propose two or three honourable men to the bailiff, and if he does not want to take any of these, he shall propose three [other candidates] to them, and if they accept one of them, it shall be fine, but if not, the bailiff shall appoint one outside these six he considers suitable ...

[Tablatt near St Gall, 1471] ... Item, the commune of Tablatt can elect and appoint a court official [*waibel*] by a majority of hands, who is also agreeable to the lord. [13: Vol. 1: 9, 139, 193, 228]

Communal constitutions rested on regular assemblies of all male householders (*Nachbarn*) and smaller executive bodies. Such councils often contained a mixture of representatives elected by the villagers (known, for example, as *Vorsteher, Heimbürge, Schöffe*) and a mayor (*Schulze, Schultheiß, Grebe* etc.) appointed by the lord or his steward. Equipped with their own institutions and resources principally derived from common lands, villagers were able to offer certain services (for instance, brewing equipment or meeting places known as *Stuben*), appoint officials (shepherds, field wardens) and to embark on joint initiatives like the purchase of lands or the 'increase of divine service', sometimes even the elevation of a local chapel into an independent parish [131]. Within the commune, decision-making was often contested. Consensus represented the accepted ideal, but diverging interests triggered fierce infighting, as in the Black Forest lordship of Hauenstein in the early eighteenth century, where 'long-term social forces that had concentrated wealth and local power within a relatively small peasant elite, despite an institutional structure designed to prevent oligarchy, combined with ... external pressures [of lords seeking to expand their authority] to produce political factions' and two decades of internal strife [137: 212]. By this point, the gap separating the largest property-holders and rural entrepreneurs from the labouring classes had widened well beyond the levels documented in the late Middle Ages. Common denominators in economic and political matters became even more difficult to find once Enlightened monarchs and landlords started to press for rationalizations and agricultural reforms.

In peripheral regions with weak or fragmented lordship, as on the German North Sea coast, rural communes could transcend the local sphere by entering into leagues (such as the peasant republic of Dithmarschen). The most spectacular example is the Swiss Confederation, where – in an unusual bridging of the town–country divide – valleys and cities forged a network of alliances between the late thirteenth and the early sixteenth century. Through a combination of purchases, political opportunism and military campaigns, the Inner Swiss cantons embarked on 'a wider struggle for emancipation [from their noble and ecclesiastical lords] which may legitimately be termed communal, in the sense of anti-feudal' [62: 389; cf. 225]. The result was not an egalitarian levelling of social differences within the federation (which increasingly distanced itself from the Empire in the wake of the Swiss/Swabian War of 1499 and effectively gained sovereignty in the Treaty of Westphalia 1648), but the establishment of a republican alternative to the predominant monarchical principle, with a potentially wider appeal. As one revolutionary tract from Upper Swabia commended in 1525:

[The Swiss] removed tyrannical power from the nobility and their other rulers, who, without mercy and contrary to all justice, had every day forced and coerced the common man with unchristian, tyrannical rapine rooted in their own pride, criminal power, and enterprise. That had to be abolished and rooted out through much war, bloodshed, and use of the sword, as is related in the Swiss chronicles and in many other reliable histories [16: 270].

The various categories of Swiss allies – ranging from full members via associates to condominiums – reflected their peculiar constitutional positions in 'histories' and pamphlets which differed from the hierarchical discourses dominating elsewhere. In the Leagues of the Grisons, a federation of Alpine communes enjoying effective autonomy after the deposition of their episcopal lord in the 1520s, political language stressed the sovereignty of the common people and extolled, at least rhetorically, the merits of quasi-democratic government, even though this unusual polity, too, was not immune to tensions caused by confessional strife and social differentiation [217; and see the discussion of chronicles in Chapter 6].

Normally, however, higher authority could not be eliminated. Complex mixtures of horizontal/communal and vertical/feudal rights created effective forms of power-sharing perhaps best described by the phrase 'communal–manorial dualism', i.e. the interaction and mutual dependency of lords and villagers. Even in the seigneurial strongholds of the eastern Empire, as we learn from a number of revisionist studies, communes could exercise considerable jurisdictional and financial competences [141: 118; 134: 650–51].

Relations with princes, lords and emperors in the early modern period

From at least the fifteenth century, the rural political matrix was complemented by a new powerful factor, the emerging state [158: Pt V]. Princes embarked on a campaign to eliminate special privileges, secure more central control and raise higher revenues to fund escalating military, administrative and representational expenses. In the periphery, this process of 'territorialization' manifested itself in a growth of regulation, taxation and 'bureaucratic' supervision. Villages used a range of strategies to negotiate such demands, ensuring that no 'single group, the German princes and their servants included, ha[d] the power to refashion rural society in the image it wanted' [144: 11]. Much of this served the interest of the village elite, but there were also 'weapons of the weak' like passive resistance, evasion or petitions (*Suppliken*) addressed to virtually anybody with influence over local affairs. The sheer volumes of these 'bottom-up' pleas for redress, favour or justice – in Hesse-Kassel, for example, relating to excessive taxation, damage by hunting or inequitable inheritance customs – resulted in institutionalized procedures and considerable grass-roots influence on territorial legislation and administration [253: 54–5].

A more formal option was participation in representative assemblies or diets. Convened by princes to raise taxes, they also presented delegates with opportunities to submit grievances and offer advice. 'The geographical extent of fully developed regimes with representation of nobles, clerics, burghers, and peasants in Central Europe reaches from Tyrol, Swabia, the Upper Rhine, the Palatinate, and the Electorate Trier through to East Frisia[, …] and thus the area of particularly highly developed towns and villages' [40: 8–9]. The extreme example of popular participation can be found in Sweden, where the peasantry formed one of the four Estates in the kingdom's *Riksdag*, the precursor of a modern parliament. With delegates elected by hundred on the principle that every independent peasant had a vote, 'it is … obvious that this was a representation very much superior to that which existed in contemporary England' [265: 70–71].

Recourse to court proceedings offered a further, if ambivalent option. On the one hand, the rise of Roman law boosted the role of university-trained professionals and eroded local custom throughout the German lands. On the other hand, legal developments presented even humble subjects with unprecedented means to seek redress for perceived injustices. Utilizing the ever expanding range of territorial jurisdiction, but also the Imperial Cameral Court established in 1495, rural communities made intensive use of central tribunals, sending delegations to – and employing advocates in – places as distant as Vienna [153]. Proceedings were costly and extremely time-consuming, but chances of an unbiased hearing often greater than in seigneurial or regional courts. This 'juridification' of conflicts in the early modern period became one of the bonds that kept the Empire together, but it also helped to establish clearer frameworks for key areas of local concern such as access to communal lands and resources [281: Ch. 5; 155].

Legal developments did not end the most dramatic form of grass-roots political pressure, open rebellion, far from it, but helped to prevent another supra-regional revolt like the Peasants' War of 1524–26. Throughout the pre-modern period, hundreds of localized risings erupted when informal and formal channels failed to solve pressing issues. The main organizational basis was the village community, whose officials often assumed a leading role, successively approaching their lords or state officials with humble requests, lists of articles, threats of disobedience and ultimately the use of violence. With the exception of the Reformation period, which inspired a revolutionary emphasis on conformity with 'divine law', legitimization derived from the dignity of ancient custom. Rural resistance was largely conservative and aimed at the prevention of higher dues and the preservation of time-honoured rights [148]. The Twelve Articles adopted by the Upper Swabian peasants in March 1525, however, additionally envisaged a new society built on communal structures, the abolition of serfdom and – in all matters spiritual and temporal – the Word of God.

> First, it is our humble plea and request ... that we should henceforth have the power and authority for the whole community to choose and elect its own pastor, and also to have the power to depose him should he conduct himself improperly
> ...
> [Third:] It has hitherto been the custom for the lords to treat us as their serfs, which is pitiable since Christ has redeemed and bought us all by shedding of his precious blood, the shepherd just as the highest, no one excepted. Therefore it is demonstrated by Scripture that we are free and wish to be free. Not that we wish to be completely free and to have no authority, for God does not teach us that. We should live according to his commandments, not the free license of the flesh ...
> ...
> Twelfth, it is our conclusion and final opinion that if one or more of the articles presented here be not in accordance with the Word of God (which we would doubt), ... then we will abandon them, when it is explained to us on the basis of Scripture [16: 253–6].

In spite of a crushing defeat in the subsequent Peasants' War and the loss of tens of thousands of lives, some of the demands were addressed indirectly and village organization survived, albeit stripped of its visionary potential.

The ensuing decades put communal bonds under enormous strain. Population growth, religious change and state building – now boosted by former Church responsibilities – all affected villages very directly. Contacts with princely and other visitations intensified, while mandates, ordinances and codifications gradually superseded local traditions. There were now two 'alternative models' of unity, 'that of the villagers and that of the administrators ... that influenced each other reciprocally' [152: 222; 235]. Within the communes, meanwhile, more inhabitants meant greater pressure on resources and growing social polarization between the largest tenants and landless labourers. Early enthusiasm for the Protestant message eroded under authoritarian 'state churches' and many communities were split down the middle. Central legislation, passed in the name of the so-called 'good police', i.e. a concerted programme aimed at preserving order and promoting the prosperity of the common weal, intervened in virtually all spheres of life and strengthened the hierarchical/patriarchal order as well as the monetarization of the rural economy. In the county of Hohenlohe (Franconia) and Upper Austria, to cite but two examples, these processes threatened the very foundations of the village commune [144: 10; 143: 125–6; 263]. Germany's princes had embarked on the road to absolutism, although they would never achieve a position which allowed them to rule without due regard to the interests of both nobles and subjects. As we will see, the early modern period also saw the emergence of theories of resistance.

The Thirty Years' War exacerbated the situation in many areas of the Empire further. Hesse-Kassel experienced demographic collapse, material destruction, brutal violence, mass emigration and 'the cumulative effect of these disruptions was to break down the cohesiveness of the village'. Yet both population levels and sociopolitical structures recovered remarkably quickly after 1648, not least because both state and seigneurial authorities bolstered village organization for their own purposes. The war became part of communal memory as one of the many factors in the everchanging character of rural society. In this sense, it underlines 'the resilience of the village in the face of the most terrifying tragedies' [152: 225–6]. While instrumentalized and increasingly exclusive, communal organization remained indispensable for the running of local affairs [154: 102].

Summary

Far from being powerless tools of seigneurial, ecclesiastical and princely interests, the rural inhabitants of the Holy Roman Empire helped to shape the world around them. The study of their villages raises difficult questions about origins, internal structures and long-term evolution in the face of demographic pressures, confessional division and state formation. Yet in many respects it echoes developments observed in Chapter 1. Chronology, size, economic power and political influence differed dramatically from those of Italian cities, of course, but the emergence of communal organization, the role in local government, the basic constitutional principles, the balancing of shared interests and inner tensions, the complex relationship with feudal lords, the significance of religion and the growing interaction with princely authorities represent shared features, not just with Italian cities, but also those in the Holy Roman Empire and indeed beyond [81; 86].

In a next step, the focus shifts to the unit of the parish; this final case study offers the chance to broaden the perspective further and to move from the secular to the ecclesiastical sphere.

3 The English Parish

The third 'ideal type' of a local community had ecclesiastical roots and an explicitly territorial character. It acquired particular significance in areas like England, where the secular 'vill' did not reach the same level of institutionalization as we have just observed for the Holy Roman Empire. There is evidence for collective action independent of the manor, the main form of English local government before the sixteenth century, but it is more patchy and informal than in German-speaking Europe [8; 116; 290]. As Max Weber noted nearly a century ago, the strength of royal jurisdiction eroded the autonomy of local associations and communities, which did not enjoy the same legislative power to regulate themselves according to sets of customary law revealed 'from within' [279: 438].

Emergence and consolidation of the parochial system

The origins of the parish date back to the High Middle Ages, when the Church developed a local network for the administration of the cure of souls, and it remains the basic unit of many Christian denominations until the present day [192; 172]. Endowed by donors with the necessary landed and financial resources, usually feudal lords but sometimes associations of neighbours, around 9,000 English places of worship acquired the canonical rights – chiefly celebration of mass, baptism and burial – associated with parochial status within clearly circumscribed boundaries (carved out of the territories of older mother churches known as 'minsters'). This gradual transformation process was under way by the first millennium and largely completed by the thirteenth century [161]. A combination of canon law restrictions and conflicting interests made the creation of new – as well as separation from old – parishes very difficult thereafter. As a result, the network remained uneven and badly equipped to adapt to changing demographic frameworks. Each parochial community maintained a clergyman with overall responsibility for all pastoral and sacramental duties – from the Fourth Lateran Council in 1215 including at least annual confession and communion by all parishioners – in return for a tenth of personal incomes (tithes), a landed estate (glebe), and customary payments for specific services. Parish priests were known either as 'rectors' – enjoying the full revenues of their benefices – or 'vicars' – receiving merely the portions conceded by external appropriators (such as colleges or religious houses [195]). The former often leased their economic assets and rights to members of the laity, with the twin consequences that rectors could become somewhat detached from their localities and that parochial benefices became highly commercialized components of the agricultural landscape, at least until the crown took statutory measures to suppress this practice in the 1520s [189: 99, 248].

Incentives for collective action derived from a set of lay duties over and above the support of the priest. According to diocesan statutes passed in the thirteenth and fourteenth centuries, parishioners had to maintain the nave and provide a long list of ornaments, service books and liturgical objects. Quite contrary to canonical expectations, based on clerical control over all church assets, these responsibilities led to the appointment of independent lay officials (churchwardens) and the emergence of resources distinct from the benefice (fabric funds), both perceptible from the late thirteenth century and widespread by about 1350 [169]. At about the same time, the doctrine of Purgatory – a posthumous soul-cleansing 'third place' for those saved from the horrors of Hell and deemed worthy to proceed to Heaven – prompted a wave of good works to minimize the period which individuals would have to spend there. Going on pilgrimages, founding of additional masses, obtaining indulgences, contributions to church finances and supporting the poor all qualified; regardless of whether pious initiatives were undertaken during people's lifetimes or commissioned by friends and families on behalf of the dead [Burgess in 207: 56–84]. In a further boost to parish consolidation, wealthy benefactors used the vehicle of 'enfeoffment to use', a legal device resembling the appointment of trustees, to augment fabric funds with landed property and thus permanent revenue. By the late Middle Ages, therefore, a fully-fledged communal infrastructure had emerged which enabled the local laity to choose representatives, supervise their activities and expand collective initiatives – for example with public works like bridge maintenance – beyond the narrowly-defined ecclesiastical sphere [184; cf. 202].

Parish government and parish records

While parishes lacked corporate status under English common law, they gained informal recognition in royal equity courts, and some even used a common seal to enhance the authority of legal documents, to claim ownership of objects and express a strong sense of collective identity. As we have seen at Gersau, it typically showed the patron saint and occasionally a legend naming the body of parishioners, as at St Mary Magdalen, Oxford [New in 165: 122–8, plates 11–12; cf. Chapter 2].

The best evidence for late medieval parish life appears in literally hundreds of sets of churchwardens' accounts surviving for England in our period. At Ashburton in Devon – a prosperous community consisting of town burghers as well as manorial tenants – parishioners made sustained efforts to increase divine service, embellish the church building and enrich their musical repertory. Resources derived from a mixture of gifts, sales, convivial events, contributions from various local bodies and revenues from landed estates. As the first surviving record for 1479–80 states (in English translation of the original Latin):

> The account of John Ferrer and John Knyghte, wardens of the parish church of St Andrew the Apostle …

> First they answer for 8 d. [old pence] of candles sold. Item for 3 d. of the gift of Henry Bonde. Item for 5½ d. of the gift of Thomasia Horsy. Item they answer for the profit on a brewing of ale sold – 31 s[hilling]. 4 d.

Information for the same year refers to additional funds (or 'stores'), administered by elected wardens on behalf of lay groups like the young men, which supported specific candles and altars in the church:

> For a perpetual remembrance there is written down in this book the sums of money of each store of the parish church of St Andrew of

Aysshperton owed by the wardens there on their account made at the accustomed days and terms in the presence of the vicar and parishioners there ... John Sparke & John Fayrmouth wardens of the goods of the store of Blessed Mary in the north aisle of the said church ... owe on their account 67 s. 2½ d. which they delivered to John Mochell & William Denbold elected wardens of the same store for the next year [25: 1, 5].

In comparative perspective, two main financial regimes can be distinguished: one, usually the preserve of wealthy metropolitan parishes in cities like London and Bristol, relied predominantly on contributions by the 'dead' (i.e. testamentary bequests of lands and tenements); the other, typically in smaller market towns and rural areas, raised funds above all from the 'living' (through voluntary collections, life-time gifts and – in a characteristic example of the interweaving of spiritual and worldly concerns – convivial church ales). Parishioners could even impose mandatory rates upon themselves [164]. Metropolitan and more peripheral parishes differed in other respects, of course, for example in the size of territory (rural clergymen in the north of the country were often in charge of vast stretches of land punctuated by semi-independent 'chapels of ease'), the degree of ecclesiastical competition (boosted by cathedrals, numerous religious houses and other parochial churches in the largest cities), the character of secular lordship (typically dominance by a gentry family in rural areas *vs* rule by an urban council) and the intensity of divine service (with high levels of benefaction fostering particularly dense liturgical calendars in wealthy city-centre parishes).

The backbone of parish government was the local householder, who made customary financial contributions and had a voice in communal assemblies. Ordinances like those at St Botolph Aldersgate, London, in 1485, made it clear that attendance at the annual audit was mandatory for anyone 'being a parysshon[er] and a householder in the same paryssh' [23] and that major decisions needed broad consensus. During a dispute over the purchase of a new silver cross at Tavistock, Devon, in 1518, for example, opponents argued that the commission had been made 'by certain persons not having the whole power or authority that to do without the assent of the whole parish' [36: 19]. Acting collectively, assemblies appointed the churchwardens, according to various systems ranging from rotation to election, received their accounts, and issued directives on the raising and allocation of funds, even though – in line with social hierarchies in the 'real' world – smaller councils composed of more 'substantial' and 'discreet' parishioners – known as the 'masters', 'feoffees', 'five/eight men' or 'vestries' – emerged from the fifteenth century. At Morebath, a tiny rural parish not far from Ashburton, the practical operation of these structures became evident during a conflict about the payment of a communal official in the 1530s. In the course of protracted negotiations, we hear of the formation of committees, of majority votes (one crucial decision being approved by 26 against 5 votes, out of a total 33 householders in the community), but also of pressure exercised by the priest as well as external bodies like diocesan and manorial authorities [170: 54–64].

Churchwardens, effectively the 'chief executives' of English parishes, came from a broadly defined 'middling' group of parishioners encompassing husbandmen, weavers, mercers and other artisans. Serving most frequently in pairs, sometimes with phased terms consisting of a year as 'junior' and another as 'senior' warden, they were respectable householders, but rarely members of the poorest sections or social elites. Like so many other local officials all over Europe, they enjoyed a certain amount of prestige and power, while negotiating conflicting expectations of neighbours, priests and the ecclesiastical hierarchy, who (in theory) visited parishes on a regular basis and administered their oaths of office. Recent research has seen them in an important 'broker' role between the communal and wider worlds of pre-modern societies [167; 166].

Parish life and parish culture

Women had no formal say in parish government – despite a handful of examples of female churchwardens like Lady Isabel Newton at Yatton in Somerset 1496–97, but they influenced communal life in many other respects. Some joined fraternities or stores supporting liturgical or spiritual activities (England even had dozens of single-sex maidens' guilds with their own assets and officers), some helped out with 'church-keeping' tasks (cleaning candlesticks, mending altar cloths and brewing), yet others shaped the spatial environment through the purchase/decoration of pews, gifts of jewellery and the erection of family monuments. Two additional, 'corporate' dimensions deserve special mention: the specifically female ritual of churching, meaning the readmission of mothers into the community after their lying-in period, and the Hocktide celebrations documented for over 40 English parishes in the week after Easter [174]. On successive days, the women and men of the parish captured members of the opposite sex for fundraising purposes, releasing them only for a ransom, a custom presenting female parishioners with an opportunity to make significant financial contributions and a chance to (temporarily) invert patterns of gender subordination. Prelates, like the Bishop of Worcester in 1450, frowned on such practices:

> ... on one set day usually, alas, when the solemn feast of Easter has ended women feign to bind men, and on another day men feign to bind women, and to do other things – would that they were not dishonourable or worse ! – in full view of passers-by, even pretending to increase church profit but earning loss [damnation] for the soul under false pretenses. Many scandals arise from the occasion of these activities, and adulteries and other outrageous crimes are committed as a clear offence to God, a very serious danger to the souls of those committing them, and a pernicious example to others [26: 553–4].

The striking enrichment of religious and ceremonial life at the close of the Middle Ages – achieved in close interaction with a host of closely related bodies like lights, guilds and chantries (i.e. local institutions established for the maintenance of candles, the organization of elaborate funerals and the support of soulmasses) – is one way in which parishes helped to shape English culture [181; 22; 19]. Another is the remarkable 'democratization' of access to the whole spectrum of fine arts. The 'great age of parish church rebuilding' and the related proliferation of perpendicular architecture and wall paintings have rightly been emphasized [church models in 172; 292], but the point has yet wider currency. The combination of pious investment, growth in clergy numbers and parochial infrastructure allowed a dramatic enhancement in musical provision, not just quantitatively, but also qualitatively: during the fifteenth century, liturgical polyphony spread well beyond royal and metropolitan contexts into hundreds of English parishes. Ashburton was among those paying for requisite manuscripts – in 1492–93 8 d 'for the Christus Resurgens at 3 partis in prykyd song' – and musicological research keeps adding ever more communities to the list. Suggestive impressions can be gained from in-situ enactments of sung services as preserved in medieval manuscripts [25: 19; 206; 300]. As recently shown for the diocese of Exeter, furthermore, highly skilled carvers worked on numerous commissions for images, bench ends, pulpits, panelled ceilings and rood screens from urban as well as rural parishes. Some communities specified their wishes in detailed contracts – as 1531 for a whole series of objects at Stratton in Cornwall – and thus participated in a complex 'elaboration' process involving constructive exchange between the latest workshop fashions and the specific needs of areas often thought to be on the cultural periphery [205]. Interdisciplinary research has started to assess how this ever-changing material environment interacted with human and atmospheric factors to create highly varied spatial experiences in English parishes, both synchronically among different individuals and diachronically across time [176; 196; 180]. A third feature is the unrivalled extension of 'political' awareness among the population at large: office-holding, elections, the auditing of accounts, legal proceedings, conflicts with lords or patrons and property management familiarized the local laity with the processes of decision-making and 'secular' government well before the Reformation and Tudor administrative reforms [Kümin in 165; 102: Ch. 7].

Political exchange was thus by no means 'parochial' in the derogatory sense of the term. Canonical obligations involved contacts with members of the ecclesiastical hierarchy, the defence of communal rights – e.g. in cases of theft, withholding of dues or disputes with contractors – required proceedings before regional and royal judges (even in Westminster's equity courts) and parishioners evolved congenial forms of multi-media communication to suit their particular needs and purposes. Face-to-face exchange naturally predominated in such tightly knit communities, be it during mass, neighbourly sociability or market transactions. Yet writing became an indispensable part of local culture, as we have already seen with regard to churchwardens' accounts (surviving from the early fourteenth century). Literacy levels were low, especially in the countryside, but clergymen, attorneys and merchants could be found to act as parochial scribes. Depending on circumstances, furthermore, communities adopted idiosyncratic auditing proceedings: some had entire sets of accounts read out to parish assemblies, others entrusted detailed scrutiny of transactions to their 'masters' or councils [173: Chs 1 and 2].

While many types of documents – deeds, inventories, lists of benefactors – served primarily archival or commemorative purposes, there is clear evidence that writing – and, from the late fifteenth century, print – actively *structured* communication processes in English parishes. Script, in other words, served not just as a medium of record, but as a *communicative* force, which prompted contemporaries to reflect on its messages and/or take responsive action. Service books shaped the ways in which priests ministered to their flocks, just as carvers' contracts affected the style and format of elaborated woodwork. Illustrating a higher level of complexity, fifteenth-century churchwardens of All Saints, Bristol, farmed property management out to estate agents. All payments the latter received – or failed to collect – were noted on copies of the parish rental, which the wardens then checked against previous years and merely summarized in their own accounts. Any discrepancies led to inquiries, legal proceedings, distraints or declarations of 'desperate debt'. In a yet more elaborate 'textual chain', ecclesiastical visitations started with a set of written questions, generated detailed protocols of individual answers, triggered follow-on proceedings for any specific issues – often requiring the gathering of additional evidence – and informed general policy decisions, the latter in turn promulgated through fresh ordinances circulated right across the diocese [185].

Reformation and early modern developments

The single biggest transformation process in the history of the English parish occurred in the Tudor period. Following primarily institutional change under Henry VIII (who broke with the papacy in 1533–34), the realm experienced a radical Protestant Reformation during the reign of Edward VI, a temporary return to Catholicism under Queen Mary in the 1550s and the gradual consolidation of the Church of England as a distinct confessional unit – which combined episcopal organization with a doctrinal emphasis on predestination – in the Elizabethan period of the later sixteenth century. From a parochial perspective, the most fundamental changes were the dismantling of the cult of saints from the mid-1530s, the 'abolition' of Purgatory in 1547 (which rendered good works irrelevant for personal salvation, removed the doctrinal basis for intercessory institutions and severed the spiritual bonds between the living and the dead), a new English liturgy from 1549, growing emphasis on preaching, and the emergence of substantial dissenting groups like the Catholic 'recusants' – who refused to attend Church of England services – and Calvinist 'puritans' – who either sought to remodel parish life along the Genevan model or drifted into separatism [171]. The archives of Long Melford, a wool church in East Anglia, document the dramatic impact on local communities. A combination of personal reminiscences, inventories of parish possessions, administrative records and official directives reveals, among other aspects, the removal of images, the suppression of a local pilgrimage and the disappearance of a whole series of liturgical rituals and convivial occasions [24]. Yet, after a few decades, the new 'prayer book' Protestantism of the Church of England could command genuine loyalty from new generations of parishioners, who appreciated the enhanced emphasis on scripture, enjoyed the congregational singing of psalms and found different ways to enhance personal involvement, for example through the foundation of lectureships [168].

Alongside, the Tudor regime reorganized English local government. The spatial focus shifted from (agricultural) vills, (feudal) manors and (royal) hundreds firmly towards the parish. Through a series of statutes starting in the 1530s and culminating in the early seventeenth century, successive parliaments appropriated its institutions to deal with secular tasks like the maintenance of the highways, the provision of men and arms for the county militia, and the relief and supervision of the poor. This brought additional opportunities for political participation for local householders, especially in the creation of the ever more significant office of the overseer of the poor, but simultaneously closer monitoring by external authorities such as justices of the peace – in a highly symbolic shift, royal arms replaced depictions of saints on church walls up and down the country – and a reinforcement of internal hierarchies, illustrated by the proliferation of select vestries monopolizing ever-larger shares of political power [149; 125; 208]. By no means all parishes went down this path, though. On the occasion of a 1636 survey of constitutional structures in the diocese of

London, some 50 communities reported the existence of oligarchic regimes, while 45 still relied on general assemblies. Among the latter, All Hallows, Lombard Street, stated that 'the busynes of our parishe is and hathe bene time out of mynde ordred by the parishioners meetinge in generall' and St Bartholomew Exchange affirmed that 'we clayme noe power by the authority of any vestry but what is agreed upon at the generall meeting of the parishioners, by the greater part of them ... and by this we have always had peace and quietness in our parish' [20].

Early modern churchwardens' accounts, vestry minutes and visitation records testify to the greater intensity of contacts with external authorities, but it was not a case of absolutist monarchs sending in armies of interfering bureaucrats. Officers remained relatively humble 'amateurs' with distinctly parochial outlooks, who balanced official duties with the traditions and priorities of their localities [191]. In certain circumstances, e.g. in the absence of powerful local gentry – as at Swallowfield, Wiltshire, where the 'chief inhabitants' drafted their own parish constitution in 1596; in churches exempt from normal diocesan jurisdiction – like the east London peculiar of Holy Trinity Minories, a (temporary) haven for Puritan preachers as well as couples wishing to marry without a formal licence or in towns like Cirencester, which had a long tradition of assertiveness against manorial lords and regional magnates, considerable room for communal manoeuvre remained [178; 203; 214; on Cirencester 102: Ch 15]. On a more modest scale, many places managed to delay the introduction of compulsory poor rates thanks to a steady stream of charitable bequests (see Figure 3) and nearly all parishes strove to minimize their financial burden by closing their boundaries to immigrants likely to fall on the communal purse. The poor law was understood as a limited support mechanism for 'deserving' recipients such as destitute widows, orphans, and people unable to work for physical reasons (in return for pious lifestyles and due deference), rather than as an entitlement of anybody struggling to make ends meet [179]. In some respects, furthermore, parliamentary statutes only generalized what local communities had trialled already, as in the case of various poor relief experiments since the fifteenth century or the introduction of new parish officials. Highway surveyors, for example, are documented in Chester from at least 1551, well before the respective law was passed at Westminster [187; 188; Alldridge in 207: 85–124].

Figure 3 Bread shelves in the collegiate church of St Mary's, Warwick. Charitable bequests by John Smith (a locally-born clergyman, d. 1624) and John Blissett (twice mayor of the town, d. 1713) allowed the parish to make weekly distributions of bread to the poor. Photo: Beat Kümin.

The impact of the 'age of plunder' – involving the sequestration of much parish property alongside all monastic, guild and chantry assets by the crown – resulted in a massive transfer of wealth from ecclesiastical institutions to secular elites, but for parishes the impact was softened by a range of evasion strategies. There is evidence of priests handing out vestments to 'good Catholic men' for safe-keeping (as at Morebath), suspiciously short inventories of communal possessions submitted to royal commissioners (as at Ashburton), churchwardens selling off the mass silver before it could be confiscated (a ploy generating capital for parish loans at Boxford in Suffolk) and local officials re-interpreting landed property as supporting charitable rather than intercessory purposes (Cratfield in Suffolk) [136: 143].

Further testimony to the resilience of communal institutions is the fact that they survived the enormous religious and social challenges of the Stuart period. Even the civil wars of the 1640s and the republican experiment in the subsequent decade, when radical Protestant denominations flourished almost unchecked, did not lead to a breakdown of parochial organization. Many aspects of worship came under attack, numerous sets of records show signs of disruption, but there was clearly no viable alternative for the entire range of the parish's pastoral, social, charitable and administrative functions. The restoration of the monarchy in 1660 reaffirmed the old religious order, and historians detect signs of continuing parish vitality well into the eighteenth century and indeed beyond [182; 199; 198]. In the long term, however, the Toleration Act of 1689, one of the outcomes of the 'Glorious Revolution', marked the beginning of the end for the parochial system. Giving substantial proportions of local inhabitants, in this case dissenting Protestants, official permission to worship in places other than the parish church, put paid to the idea of an inclusive ecclesiastical community. What continued to bind local inhabitants thereafter were social and political rather than spiritual ties. An entirely different concept of local government only arrived with the new poor law of 1834 in the Victorian period.

Summary

The parish was the most significant communal unit in pre-modern England. Nearly all inhabitants belonged to one of the 9,000 components of a network which had ecclesiastical roots, but soon expanded into the social, cultural and political spheres. Quasi-corporate status, independent fabric funds, rating powers and representative government – based on principles like election, accountability and collective interests (albeit with a clear bias towards those of local elites) – were the product of lay initiatives taken in the late Middle Ages, and provided firm bases for the articulation of a parish voice in all dealings with Church and state. Canon law and royal jurisdiction proved too strong for a genuinely 'Weberian' legislative autonomy, but parishioners managed to carve out considerable room for manoeuvre. Neither the sixteenth-century Reformations nor the seventeenth-century revolutions led to the breakdown of parochial organization, in large measure due to formal local government responsibilities added during the Tudor reigns. These socio-political transformations brought no sudden 'incorporation' into the realm, but a growth in secular-administrative preoccupations and more intense interactions with regional and central authorities. Adaptation and resilience appear as the underlying themes throughout the centuries. The reliance on 'amateur' officials and locally generated revenues ensured that communal experience remained a feature of English life until the Victorian age and, in the form of surviving 'parish council' powers, even to the present day.

PART II Local Communities in Comparative Perspective

Following the regional and typological case studies sketched in Part I, the focus now turns to comparative analysis. What were the main features of local communities in pre-modern Europe? How did they evolve over time? What was their relationship with other local, regional and central bodies? Chapters 4 and 5 integrate the evidence emerging from Italian cities, German villages and English parishes on the one hand and move towards a more general characterization of the 'communal age' on the other.

4 Communal Cultures

The significance of the communal phenomenon can be illustrated in very concrete terms: there were some 500 English towns by the mid-fourteenth century, at least 50,000 parishes in the Holy Roman Empire at the close of the Middle Ages and literally hundreds of thousands of villages throughout early modern Europe. Even within the same region or time-period, however, each and every one of these had a distinct history and profile, which prevents simple generalizations [100: 15; 163; 135: 136]. Any attempt to identify basic building blocks, common structural features and long-term trends must thus be undertaken with due acknowledgement of numerous exceptions and contrasting developments. Communal culture was made up of many components: in what follows, we will concentrate on aspects of community formation, membership, inner coherence/divisions, resources, values, political life and communication patterns.

Community formation

When and how local communities came into existence provides a first indication of the enormous variety across space and time. In principle, of course, towns, villages and parishes could emerge at any point in time, as a result of forces like colonization, missionary activity, settlement policy, economic development, local initiative or environmental change [139; 193]. Yet there is a very notable clustering of examples after the first millennium, especially between *c.* 1100 and 1300. The high Middle Ages witnessed the coming together of a number of contributing factors: the commercial revolution feeding into a surge in town foundations (especially along the urban belt stretching from north-western Europe to northern

Italy); a shift from demesne farming under direct seigneurial control towards the co-ordinated agricultural production of independent peasant producers (e.g. in the Holy Roman Empire); and the universal pastoral offensive of the Christian Church aimed at securing the administration of sacraments to each and every individual. The reconstruction of the exact chronology requires painstaking regional research – as recently conducted for the emergence of the rural commune in the twelfth-century Tuscan plains around Lucca, with areas like northern Scandinavia or Eastern Europe likely to reveal a later initiation and completion date [91; 40: 2–4; 59; 156]. It has traditionally been argued that the constitution of a new socio-political unit required a tangible sign or ritual such as the swearing of an oath by all associates (*coniuratio*), but in many cases progress was too gradual or consciousness not sufficiently developed for such a spectacular moment to be arranged, or, indeed, recorded. In any case, the principle of territorial organization – 'pioneered' and most fully realized by the parish – introduced a new, 'advanced' feature into societies normally structured in line with the personal bonds created by kinship and feudal relations [177; 297].

One striking feature is the interaction and mutual reinforcement of parallel processes, especially in the countryside. Spiritual-ecclesiastical and secular-economic impulses often combined to boost communalization. Shared responsibilities in terms of church maintenance could boost levels of co-operation in some medieval villages, just as the existence of economic collaboration led to aspirations for independent parochial structures elsewhere [132: 105; 129: Ch. 2]. On the other hand, of course, examples for tensions between different strands – e.g. where several independent settlements formed part of the same parish – can also be found. As has been observed for the Florentine territory: 'At times [spiritual] ties were synonymous with the political units ..., but more often, they transcended and contradicted the established patterns of inter-communal relationships' [135: 137]. A second remarkable characteristic of community-formation is the contribution of feudal lords and ecclesiastical rulers alongside local initiatives. By means of town/village foundations or imposition of parochial dues, nobles and church authorities furthered their own interests, but – perhaps ironically – sowed the seeds for greater local autonomy at the same time. As we have seen in the preceding case studies, the emergence of permanent institutions, fund-raising mechanisms and communal identities had the potential for dynamic evolution well beyond the original purposes. The complex character of such 'external relations' will have to be examined in more detail in Chapter 5.

Membership

Who belonged to a local community? The answer to this fundamental question is not as straightforward as may be expected. In the most basic definition, all of the inhabitants of the respective topographical units counted as villagers, burghers and parishioners. Such an inclusive view was reflected, for example, by clergymen reporting on the number of souls in their congregations or by local officials compiling early population statistics in the Age of Enlightenment. Yet for many practical purposes, local society was subdivided by a wide range of criteria, most obviously by age (14 being a common transition point into adulthood), gender (women counting as the subordinate sex in a patriarchal system), personal status (expressed in variables such as freedom/serfdom, landholding, wealth, education and clientelage) and legal affiliation (some individuals/groups answered to different jurisdictional or personal lords than their neighbours). 'Politically', i.e. in the sense of having rights of participation in decision-making, entitlement varied most dramatically. The extremes range from near-universal adult (male) franchises – as for example in the general assemblies of rural Swiss cantons (*Landsgemeinden*) – to highly aristocratic systems based on a very narrow pool of privileged elites – most notably in the exclusive republic of Venice.

Qualification for full membership was conveyed by a community-specific selection of common requirements: usually headship of a household (understood not just as the dwelling place of a nuclear family, but as the basic building block of pre-modern society serving a wide range of economic and cultural functions within its own 'precinct of peace' [40: Ch. 1]), alongside the right to bear arms, an ability to meet financial obligations and subscription to a set of values / beliefs or constitutional principles. Depending on status and stage in the life-cycle, the moment of access could be determined by coming-of-age, inheritance, marriage or payment of an entry fee, while loss of the respective privileges might ensue from relocation, banishment, transgression of rules, conversion or military defeat [42/vol. 2: Chs 5–6; 276]. Possession of full communal rights, however, did not necessarily translate into power. The extent of actual influence depended on variables like the number of similarly qualified members, the presence or absence of nobles / prelates and the position of the community within the larger political landscape. For towns within the Holy Roman Empire, for example, integration into a principality (as a *Landstadt*) meant much more restricted autonomy than direct subordination under the Emperor (as a *Reichsstadt*), villagers in increasingly 'absolutist' monarchies like France faced stronger interference than those in decentralized republics, while the existence of a resident gentleman restricted the room for manoeuvre of English parishes.

Communal bonds

Zooming in on inner structures, how coherent could such heterogeneous organisms be? The differing contexts and the dynamics of membership are but two factors impacting on their strength. 'Community', as Peter Burke has observed in relation to language groups, is 'at once an indispensable term and a dangerous one', since 'it seems to imply a homogeneity, a boundary and a consensus that are simply not to be found when one engages in research at ground level' [44: 5]. We thus have to distinguish between a 'communal will' as enshrined in, say, laws and court verdicts, and the protracted negotiation of differing individual/factional pressures which preceded them. These contrasting perspectives are not incompatible, but effectively two sides of the same coin.

There is ample evidence for the solidity of internal ties: common economic interests (e.g. in open-field agriculture), shared heritage (celebrated in chronicles, visual representations and increasingly sophisticated archives), collective sociability (as during seasonal festivities) and rituals marking key moments in civic life (such as the staging of general assemblies or the elections of officials [171: Ch. 4; 133; 46; 305]). Religion arguably provided the strongest incentives, through the practice of common worship, the Christian ideal of charity and, in Catholic contexts, the efficacy of corporate intercession. In the Bristol parish of All Saints on the eve of the

Reformation, the community commemorated its benefactors once a year in a dedicated ceremony known as the 'General Mind', as evident from a note in the church book and from dedicated payments in the wardens' accounts:

> Where it has been a laudable custom of long continuance used, that on ... the Sunday before Ash Wednesday, the names of good doers and wellwillers by whom livelode – tenements, buildings, jewels, books, chalices, vestments and with divers other ornaments and goods ... – has been given unto the church unto the honour and worship of almighty God and increasing divine service, to be rehearsed and shown yearly unto you by name, ... that they shall not be forgotten but be had in remembrance and be prayed for of all this parish that be now and all of them that be to come, ... that by the infinite mercy of almighty God, by the intercession of our blessed lady and of all blessed saints of heaven, in whose honour and worship this church is dedicated, [they] may come to everlasting bliss and joy ... AMEN.
>
> ....
> [1463–64 account] Payments
> ....
> Item for the General Mind – 10s 8 ½d. [22/Part 1: 4, 103]

In the north German city of Bremen, to add a 'secular' example, the following oath had to be sworn by all native and newly admitted burghers from 1365 until the early nineteenth century:

> I will obey the council and never oppose it; also be true and faithful towards the council, burghers and the city as a whole in all dangers and hardship which this good commune may face now and in the future; neither will I cause or support any uproar, but faithfully report to the council any unrest or covert practices aimed against this good city; and I will uphold the law books newly established by concord, as sworn by the council and commonality; I will pay my right dues and taxes ... and I will promote what is best for the council and city as a whole, as well as prevent any damage and disadvantage, as far as I possibly can ... So help me God! [288]

Civic oaths symbolize the subordination of individual under collective interests, even though explicit references to 'unrest' and the need for obedience suggest that this was more easily proclaimed than achieved. Indeed, it has been argued that members of 'scattered' communities find it easier to share abstract values – due to the absence of tensions and conflicts in everyday life – than townspeople or villagers who lived in proximity to each other [51: 22].

Inner tensions

The special interests of members, sub-groups and factions undoubtedly posed the greatest threat to communal harmony. As we know from Renaissance scholarship, in particular, the role of the individual increased over the course of the period studied here. In interrelated developments first observed in late medieval northern Italy, but soon across the wider Continent, growing self-awareness found expression in, for instance, actively commissioned portrait paintings, enhanced social mobility due to better education, increasing resort to reasoning and experimentation, greater emphasis on personal conscience, and the rise of private property and entrepreneurial initiative as a feature of the gradual evolution from feudalism to capitalism [237; 242]. As has been shown, religion could act as a strong bond, but its very force also divided localities wherever the doctrinal consensus broke down, be it through the emergence of 'heretical' groups like the Cathars, Waldensians, Lollards or Hussites, the post-Reformation multiplication of denominational strands, or the growth of scepticism, religious apathy and even atheism. There were, in other words, always community members who openly or secretly diverged from the orthodox line; at times, their numbers became significant enough to cause genuine disruption: in polities like the Swiss Confederation, the Holy Roman Empire, France, the Netherlands and England, even periods of civil war.

Ancestry and lineage, to move to secular tensions, mattered not just in noble circles and princely courts; almost everyone felt a primary allegiance to family and wider kin. The power and influence of the respective groups varied dramatically, in line with factors like wealth, length of residence and marriage alliances. In landholding registers, tax records or council minutes, certain surnames are invariably more prominent than others. An extreme case of a local dynasty can be found in the Swiss micro-republic of Gersau we have already encountered. The Camenzind family, consisting of three interrelated lines, first appeared among the free men who exchanged pastoral land with a neighbouring monastery in 1345 (i.e. one of the earliest documents of collective initiative in the village); lost one of their members fighting against the Habsburgs at the battle of Sempach in 1386; occupied countless secular and ecclesiastical offices – including mayoral positions – throughout the centuries of local sovereignty from 1390 to 1798; figured among the pioneers of proto-tourism (as owners of the Gersauer Hof inn) as well as early industrialization (as silk manufacturers and traders) in the late 1700s; and even produced Gersau's most distinguished local historian of the nineteenth century [122]. At the time of writing in 2011, the Camenzinds remain similarly conspicuous, with – to give just a few examples – Oscar (a former world cycling champion) serving as the local postman, Marzell looking after the district archive, Nicole and Mathias running a silk mill in the fifth generation, butcher René acting as *Röllivater* (headman of the influential carnival guild) and Josef taking care of the district council's finances. Alongside, only a handful of other families – the Baggenstoss, Küttel, May, Müller, Niederer, Nigg, Rigert, Schöchli and Waad families– enjoyed full burgher rights in the pre-modern period. In fact, disagreements about whether the Küttels should be stripped of their citizenship threw the commune into its biggest constitutional crisis in the early seventeenth century [250/Vol. iii: 181–2; 12: GST; www.gersau.ch]. The negotiation of often-conflicting demands of family interests, local custom, religious norms and communal priorities in the face of limited resources and external pressures required a high degree of political astuteness, making the Camenzinds' enduring prominence all the more remarkable.

Much better-known, of course, is the significance of kinship ties and rivalries in Italian cities. As symbolized by the formidable towers of leading nobles, which punctuate the skyline of medieval towns like San Gimignano in Tuscany, communities often found their affairs overshadowed by struggles within the elite. This involved political conflicts over precedence and positions, sometimes erupting in violent confrontations and prolonged feuds. When the so-called 'Black Guelfs' rose to power in early fourteenth-century Florence, prominent members of the rival faction of the 'White Guelfs' had to leave the city, as we can read in a family chronicle from 1312:

> I, Neri Alfieri dello Strinato Raminghi [member of the Strinati, a family of Florentine magnates] in order to memorialize those things which

have happened, will write about the facts of my family as they have really and personally transpired, and will begin in the year 1312 ... I, Neri, am in the city of Padua with all my family, as a man banished from Florence for what is now ten years, because of that treacherous tyrant [Charles of Valois, brother of the King of France]. And due to his arrival in Florence and because of the deceitful Black Guelfs, many other Ghibellines and White Guelfs, both magnates and *popolo*, were banished along with me ... On 2 November [1301], the citizens of Florence, that is the Ghibellines and the White Guelfs, were robbed, and the suburbs were robbed and burned ... by these people. The men ..., with a group of armed soldiers, came to our house ... and stole all they found there; fortunately the night before we had hidden all of the most expensive things [5: 87–8].

Viewed from this angle, an urban community was – as Edward Muir has put it – 'less an abstract moral entity than the public representation of private arrangements', where local institutions structured exchanges to suit factional interests and officials answered to powerful patrons rather than the common good. On the other hand, communes often closed ranks against outsiders. When Knight Angelo, a feudal lord from the region, tried to arrest Costantino Rizzardi at a tavern in Buia near Udine in the Friuli in 1516, the latter successfully appealed to his fellow citizens with the words: 'Oh my commune, help me, now'. This provoked a gathering of fifty local inhabitants, forced the noble to abandon his plan and prompted the burghers to agree a general policy for such situations at a subsequent town meeting [96: 6 and 1–2].

Alongside kinship allegiance, social inequality posed perennial challenges to communal harmony. Some constitutions cemented professional segmentation by giving trade guilds a formal role in town government, meaning that membership in these largely self-governing associations became a precondition of political participation. Given the principle of householder-rule, younger and poorer men found it generally more difficult to influence local policy than large landowners and wealthy traders. While the former welcomed moves towards wider participation and a more equitable distribution of resources, the latter tended to defend the status quo and to aim for closer association with regional and central elites. In these circumstances, external bodies had the chance to drive wedges between different groups in towns and villages. A prominent example is the process of social polarization in the English village of Terling from the late sixteenth century. Members of the upwardly mobile 'middling sort', infused with the religious and moral ideas of Puritan ministers, started to distance themselves from less prosperous neighbours. The latter, rightly or wrongly suspected of a fondness for alehouse-haunting and questionable morals, appeared as unfit companions on the road towards a godly community. Two concepts of order confronted each other: one based on reformed standards of sobriety and social discipline, the other more in line with traditional popular culture [157]. In Chapter 2 we came across a comparable eighteenth-century example from the Black Forest, where the rise of a relatively small peasant elite prevented the villagers from presenting a united front against seigneurial encroachments [137: 212]. And yet in spite of all social inequalities and group divisions, as a long-term survey of the English town of Cirencester underlines, historians are often able to detect an overarching – if continuously renegotiated – communal personality with a 'mind of its own' [102].

Gender constituted a further fault line within local communities. Biblical, legal and humoral discourse invariably portrayed men as the superior sex. Due to their allegedly weaker constitution and greater propensity to temptation, women lacked political rights and occupied a subservient role in pre-modern households. While involvement in certain trades, even to the extent of heading a workshop, had been possible in the late Middle Ages, the twin forces of demographic pressure – which boosted the number of men looking for work – and Reformation doctrine – which idealized marriage and motherhood as the 'natural' estates for women – reduced such opportunities and reinforced patriarchal control. As seen in the German case study, recent research identifies the social capital generated by male-dominated guilds and communal institutions as an important factor in this process of marginalization [280: 104–6, 186–95; 260: 332–4, 340–44].

Yet the notion of systemic and ever growing discrimination may present too bleak an assessment of women's roles in local society. Gender inequalities, for a start, were a general – rather than specifically communal – characteristic of pre-modern Europe and once we consider informal spheres of influence, the picture becomes more nuanced. The case study of the English parish reveals considerable female presence in the public sphere, be it through regular church attendance, negotiation of seating arrangements, pious benefaction or involvement in seasonal festivities like church ales and hocking. The Reformation closed off some avenues – especially office-holding in religious guilds and 'career opportunities' in religious houses, but opened up others – like (at the lower social end) rudimentary education in catechism classes, (in the middling ranks) the chance to shape communal culture as a clergyman's wife and (further up the scale) the endowment of lectureships and other forms of religious patronage. Even a pillar of male prerogative like jurisdiction could be instrumentalized: according to Bernese ecclesiastical records, women enlisted local consistory courts to enforce Reformation ideals by punishing drunkards, adulterers and work-shy husbands, sometimes drawn from amongst the tribunal's own members. By the eighteenth century, the confident use of legal channels can be interpreted as a sign of emancipation [197: 318–19]. More generally still, women acted as arbitrators of reputations, denouncing individuals deemed to have overstepped the boundaries of custom and respectability. The power of persistent rumour and gossip about dishonesty or the inability to control a wife could undermine the personal honour of high-ranking men, while shaming rituals like rough music or charivari ridiculed victims in a most public and humiliating manner. Whether by personal conviction, or as unwitting instruments of patriarchal suppression, women thus played an instrumental part in the preservation of norms about sexual decency and gender relations [239]. Yet to envisage 'women' as a homogeneous group would be as misleading as to speak of early modern 'men': while gender was an important part of their identities, so were numerous other components like social status, religious orientation, regional setting and place of residence, resulting in a complex matrix of shared experiences and individual differences [273].

Other inner tensions were of a topographical nature. Many subunits like wards, quarters, neighbourhoods, streets and chapelries developed identities of their own. Be it for reasons of economic specialization, particular social profiles, military functions, delegated administrative powers or independent cultural traditions, members could view themselves as distinct from those of other parts of the same settlement. Local pride fostered the embellishment of representative buildings, especially churches, inns and guild halls, sometimes with a blatantly competitive edge, while on ritual occasions like carnival relations between communal sub-units could escalate from friendly banter via verbal threats to violent confrontation. Since the mid-seventeenth century, rivalries within the city of Siena have culminated twice yearly during the Palio, a spectacular horse race on the vast Piazza del Campo, where ten riders – clad in the respective colours and symbols – compete to achieve victory for their district (*contrado*; www.ilpalio.org). Where they had their own assemblies, patron saints, officials, resources or duties relating to local infrastructure, public safety and the collection of dues, neighbourhoods could follow their own agendas and political objectives. In the medieval city of Cologne, territorial units with close links to parishes carried out administrative tasks like the keeping of property registers for their quarters (*Schreinsbücher*) and retained a degree of independence from the communal council [73b: 138, 147–9; 194; 160]. The range and significance of activities at this level continued to shape identities throughout the early modern period, as demonstrated notably in the case studies of the Ribera district of Barcelona and neighbourhood ties in late eighteenth-century Paris [68b; 82a]. During the German Peasants' War of 1524–26, to highlight potentially destabilizing effects on larger units, radical ideas from the countryside infiltrated towns via their suburbs, where occupational groups, such as the gardeners' guild at Strasbourg or the vintners' guild at Heilbronn, and individual labourers retained close ties with the agricultural world. Suburbs, of course, were often physically as well as symbolically demarcated from the more prosperous central areas by means of the town wall [39: 101–2].

As in all other forms of social organization, however, there is evidence for coherence as well as frictions within such sub-units. Illustrating the former, over four-fifths of seventeenth-century Southwark inhabitants found marriage partners within their own suburb; there is strong evidence for mutual assistance; and a relatively wide spectrum of householders served in local offices throughout the seventeenth century. In this sense, England's capital 'may be conceived of more fruitfully as a mosaic of neighbourhoods than as one single amorphous community' [71: 293]. On the other hand, as recently documented for late medieval Zurich and early modern Münster, interpersonal relations were soured by myriads of petty squabbles – over stinking pigsties, disputed property-boundaries, rights of access or broken contracts; many of which escalated from personal confrontations via informal arbitration attempts to civil litigation in the local law courts [108; 146].

All in all, sub-units had the potential to acquire distinct profiles, but oscillated between many of the same ties and tensions as the overarching local community they remained a part of.

Resources and revenues

The assets of medieval villages in northern and western Europe consisted mostly of common lands like meadows and forests, although their size, use, legal frameworks, administration and long-term fortunes varied from region to region. Access mattered above all for the less prosperous inhabitants, whose livelihoods depended on allocations of free firewood, building materials and pasture for livestock. By the early modern period, such rights tended to be eroded, either because of more restrictive by-laws agreed by the communes or agricultural associations themselves (in thinly veiled attempts to safeguard the interests of members against the ever-growing numbers of landless labourers) or a gradual process of 'privatization' (specifically enclosure promoted by proto-capitalist groups like the English gentry who sought to intensify the pastoral economy). In the Netherlands and parts of south-western Germany, however, communal lands remained relatively extensive well into the nineteenth century [124]. Parishes, as we have seen in Chapter 3, financed their operations through a community-specific mixture of active fundraising mechanisms like voluntary collections, seasonal celebrations and mandatory rates on the one hand, and endowments of lands and tenements on the other [cf. most recently 28]. Depending on circumstances, rural as well as urban communities could derive additional income from court fines; fees for the use of shared facilities like baking houses or breweries; rents for drinking halls, bathing houses or mills and a wide range of further services.

By far the biggest assets accumulated in large, autonomous urban environments. As early as 1262, a detailed list of the 'communal goods and possessions' of Vicenza in northern Italy included real estate (among which three palaces), towers and houses within the walls, lands and jurisdictional rights in the surrounding territory, feudal revenues from a number of villages, rural castles, forests and scattered further property [1]. Republics like Nuremberg or Venice reached revenue levels rivalling those of major principalities. The

Swiss city state of Bern owed its prosperity to extensive landed possessions (acquired through a combination of purchase, treaties or conquest), feudal incidents, customs fees and excise payments, complemented by large-scale appropriations of church property during the Reformation, allowing the council to embark on a process of 'state building without taxation' and, by the eighteenth century, to invest substantial sums in foreign capital markets [Kapossy in 227; 68a].

Communal values

Living in close proximity, belonging to the same estate and reliance on regular co-operation fostered a distinct communal ethic. Not everybody shared each component in equal measure at all times, but some general guidelines emerge strongly from the sources. For most of pre-modern Europe, Christianity provided the pervasive spiritual framework. Both before and after the Reformation, attendance at church was expected, God's wrath feared, and adherence to universal norms like the Ten Commandments undisputed. While individual beliefs came to differ between the various confessional groups, 'brotherly love', a spirit of neighbourliness and an 'ethic of empathy' remained congenial ideals for communal society [244: 28; 178: 836; 40: Chs 4–5]. In contrast to members of the first and second estates, furthermore, burghers and villagers strove to communalize their Church, ideally to a point where councils supervised all endowments, the encroachments of ecclesiastical courts receded, and congregations appointed their own clergy. Corporate lay control brought reliable and affordable access to religious instruction and sacramental provision on the one hand, and the opportunity to turn a locality into a 'sacral community' on the other. In some areas, this required the Reformation-enabled erosion of ecclesiastical powers, in others – like German Imperial Free Cities or the Swiss rural cantons – considerable progress had already been made in the late Middle Ages [94; 120].

Another set of ideals – composed of the right of 'subsistence', the preservation of 'peace', 'equality' before the law, the pursuit of the 'common good' and the aspiration to personal 'freedom' – were of a more secular nature [42/Vol. 1: Ch. 3]. Most fundamentally, communal society believed that each household was entitled to a livelihood. While resigned to the fact that the fruits of their labour were subject to customary feudal and ecclesiastical dues, subjects felt strongly that these could not be increased to a level which deprived families of the basic means of existence. Where that threshold was crossed, resistance became legitimate. Within premodern 'popular culture' we find a time-honoured way of thinking fundamentally opposed to the emerging belief in the absolute nature of property (conveying owners the right to do whatever they liked with 'private' lands) and committed to the principle of a 'moral economy' (in which members of the social elites had to live up to their paternalistic rhetoric [213; 275]). Members of the third estate also prioritized 'peace' and the 'rule of law' over the waging of war. Despite valuing the right to bear arms as an attribute of masculinity and personal freedom, commoners derived their identity from professional honour and personal honesty rather than military glory. Noble feuds and external attacks posed real threats to their vulnerable settlements and limited possessions, while discord undermined communal harmony from the inside. Ideally, conflicts needed to be solved by neighbourly reconciliation, informal mediation or – as a last resort – legal action, if possible involving *local* judges. This did not always materialize in practice, of course (not least because some communes embarked on aggressive territory-building of their own), but yet more than other political authorities of the time, town and village councils derived their legitimacy from the ability to uphold peace and the rule of law. Many urban oaths and statutes explicitly required burghers not to seek justice elsewhere. This is one element that the Leveller movement picked up during the English revolution. Pushing more generally for a wider franchise, periodic parliaments and a radical decentralization of government at the crucial juncture when the monarchy was (temporarily) abolished, their *Agreement of the Free People of England* (1649) called for exclusively *communal* jurisdiction. No external body should 'continue or make a law, for any other way of Judgements, or Conviction of life, limb, liberty, or estate, but onely by twelve sworn men of the Neighbor-hood; to be chosen in some free way by the people' [34: 326].

As illustrated by the passage 'I will promote what is best for the council and city as a whole, as well as prevent any damage and disadvantage' in Bremen's city oath, pursuit of the 'common good' constitutes another pillar of communal ideology. Hardly any mandate or statute omitted it from the preamble. This 'corporate' ethos again differs from the nobility's emphasis on personal distinction, dynastic interest and status privilege. The chief source of inspiration came from local oaths rather than Antique philosophy or scholastic theology, where the 'common good' was also intensely debated. In the course of the late Middle Ages (and thus the formative period of local communities), the pledge to 'further the lord's advantage and shield him from any detriment', a standard feature of homage ceremonies, was refocused away from an individual to a collective point of reference. What mattered now was the prosperity of towns, villages and parishes as a whole, what needed to be resisted where detrimental activities like hoarding, profiteering, violations of custom and the erosion of liberties. Adopted first in fifteenth-century urban mandates as the justification of more sustained regulation of local affairs, the ideal was then appropriated by the early modern 'police state' to justify its own efforts to control ever more areas of public life. In this way, 'communes played a very significant part in the evolution of the common good' as a legitimizing tool for authorities throughout early modern Europe, from the Holy Roman Empire to the Iberian peninsula [42/Vol. 1: 103; 78: 47].

A final communal value to note is the long-term aspiration towards personal freedom. In some regions of Europe – like England, the Swiss Confederation and Sweden, serfdom had largely disappeared by the start of the early modern period. For reasons varying from greater commercialization of agriculture and colonization via the foundation of towns to collective purchases of rights of freedom, individuals and groups managed to rid themselves of much-resented servile attributes like restrictions of marriage partners, limited personal mobility and death-duties known as 'heriot'. In 1390, as seen in Chapter 2, the parishioners of Gersau in present-day Switzerland – represented by their mayor and three other notables – paid the patrician family von Moos of Lucerne the princely sum of £690 for the entire range of feudal rights over the local community and its inhabitants:

> To all seeing or hearing this charter, we [several members of the von Moos family], Burghers of Lucerne, having received the jurisdiction and dues of Gersau from the Lords of Habsburg, proclaim that we have sold [the said rights], for us and our heirs, ... to the honourable people

Ruedin Truochfelder, currently mayor of Gersau, Jenni Heintzen, Heini Kamenzint [Camenzind], und Jenni Megger of Gersau, on behalf of themselves and the commonality of others of Gersau, ... for the sum of £690. Thus we have acquitted ourselves ... of the same jurisdiction and dues and reserve nothing for ourselves or our heirs, pronouncing the above said of Gersau commonly and individually and all their heirs free, quit and released with this charter ... . We also profess in good faith to observe this sale and the contents of this letter in perpetuity, never to do anything against it [12: Charter no. 6].

Another route was active resistance. We have already noted that this was normally sparked by violations of custom and time-honoured rights, but there were exceptions. One of the most spectacular examples, the English Peasants' War of 1381, startled ruling elites with calls for the abolition of serfdom. According to the chronicler Thomas Walsingham, the priest John Ball had roused the rebels with a very powerful appeal:

'Whan Adam dalf, and Eve span, Wo was thanne a gentilman?' And continuing his sermon, he tried to prove by the words of the proverb that he had taken for his text, that from the beginning all men were created equal by nature, and that servitude had been introduced by the unjust and evil oppression of men, against the will of God, who, if it had pleased Him to create serfs, surely in the beginning of the world would have appointed who should be a serf and who a lord. Let them consider, therefore, that He had now appointed the time wherein, laying aside the yoke of long servitude, they might, if they wished, enjoy their liberty so long desired. Wherefore they must be prudent, hastening to act ...; first killing the great lords of the realm, then slaying the lawyers, justices and jurors, and finally rooting out everyone whom they knew to be harmful to the community in the future. So at last they would obtain peace and security, if, when the great ones had been removed, they maintained among themselves equality of liberty and nobility, as well as of dignity and power [11: 374–5].

Moving to the Holy Roman Empire, the vision of 'turning Swiss', i.e. following the model of self-governing city states like Zurich or Bern and rural republics like Uri, Schwyz and Unterwalden, complemented – from the age of the Reformation – by the evangelical emphasis on the 'freedom of a Christian' (which many commoners seamlessly extended to the socio-political realm), inspired protest movements to fight for – if not outright liberation – then the easing of obligations: hence the third of the Twelve Articles drawn up at Memmingen during the Peasants' War in 1525 argued that 'it is demonstrated by Scripture that we are free and wish to be free'. Given the fierce opposition to such radical change by the feudal powers, rebels usually obtained no more than quasi-constitutional fixations of customary law. These often included partial improvements like shifts from temporary to inheritable tenures and reductions in death duties and labour services. Over the course of the early modern period, reflecting a wider trend towards the 'juridification' of conflicts, a growing proportion of protests came to be channelled into legal proceedings. Instead of planning armed campaigns, peasants and burghers now instructed lawyers to argue their case in court, if need be at regional, territorial and even imperial level [72; 16: 252–7; 10; 158: Ch. V].

Political life in local communities

Within the realm of politics, communal values translated into the closely related and, in many ways, remarkably 'modern' principles of broad participation, elections, fixed terms of office and general accountability. Fundamental business relating to the swearing of oaths, constitutional change or going to war usually required the calling of general assemblies of all members, while day-to-day government lay in the hands of smaller bodies like councils and vestries. It is worth re-emphasizing that local communities exercised quasi-state powers through legislation (by the passing of mandates, ordinances, articles etc.), jurisdiction (enforcing secular/ecclesiastical laws through town and village courts or parish consistories [29]) and administration (via the collection of dues, management of property, allocation of resources and other 'bureaucratic' tasks). The way these responsibilities were carried out, another aspect which deserves signalling here, evolved out of local solutions to practical problems rather than any learned blueprint or 'enlightened' political theory.

Communal positions were allocated on the criteria of shared obligations and/or merit rather than personal or dynastic entitlement. Throughout the case studies examined in Part 1 we have seen that elections were very commonly used in towns, villages and parishes. Very early evidence outside of Italy survives for the *jurés* of Valenciennes, in present-day Belgium, from 1114 [4: 129]. Great effort was invested in the regulation of eligibility, franchises, procedure and ceremonial, as the most sought-after positions conveyed considerable power and prestige. To manage the ever-present risks of corruption or oligarchization, elaborate systems emerged, especially in urban environments. Some cities like eighteenth-century Bern even introduced an element of chance, like the drawing of lots, to prevent monopolization by certain factions or family groups. Through such measures, as well as the continuing influence of trade guilds (and the latent pressures of protest and/or reform movements), participation could remain relatively extensive – although never 'democratic' in the modern, universal sense – throughout the early modern period. Similar observations have been made for the countryside, even in regions like Bohemia, where feudal lordship remained strong [104; 142]. This system worked, because civic service formed as important a part of republican identity as military defence, ensuring that even busy merchants and master craftsmen felt obliged to take the time to act as aldermen and mayors [67: 56–68]. The filling of lower, unpaid, yet onerous offices like constables or overseers of the poor, on the other hand, could be more difficult. Many English villages and parishes introduced high fines for elected members who declined to serve. During an acrimonious financial dispute in 1646, for example, no fewer than three parishioners of Great St Mary's, Cambridge, preferred to pay a hefty 40 s penalty each rather than to accept their election as churchwardens [18: 1646].

Other 'advanced' features, compared to feudal, princely and especially absolutist regimes, were the limited terms of appointment and the general accountability of all representatives. At the end of their turn, usually after a year, officials had to answer to the community's sovereign body, often with written reckonings of all items of income and expenditure. Audit procedures, involving the scrutiny of supporting documentation and a comparison with customary practice, reduced the dangers of embezzlement and personal enrichment. As highlighted in Chapter 3, entire series of such records can be found in European archives, providing unrivalled insights into communal operations [184: 82–102].

Communication and representation

In recent times, scholarly priorities have moved from 'hard' social, economic and political history towards 'softer' topics like the display/perception of power in particular and the analysis of communication cultures in general. Pioneering studies examined the public rituals and ceremonies of Italian cities, revealing how processions of communal officers along carefully selected routes helped contemporaries to imagine towns not just as physical and social entities, but also as distinct political spaces. [258: 235; 111: 213–14]. Just like the swearing of communal oaths, or indeed the holding of public executions, such spectacular events not only 'reflected' a given political order, but helped to 'constitute' it in the first place. Artists have provided us with imaginative depictions of civic ceremonial; one famous Renaissance example is Gentile Bellini's 'Procession in St Mark's Square' of 1496, in which an elaborately structured line-up of clergymen, government officials, confraternity members, burghers and musicians celebrate a religious feast at the heart of the Republic of Venice, but similar occasions were staged by communities in other contexts and periods (see Figure 4). Research in this area thus requires greater sensitivity to contemporary media use and refined methical tools to decode the structures and meanings of symbolic communication.

Engagement with these issues has been particularly intense in German-speaking Europe, boosted by a number of interdisciplinary research clusters [305]. Of particular interest for local community studies are conceptualizations advanced by Rudolf Schlögl for pre-modern towns. As members of what he calls 'presence societies' (*Anwesenheitsgesellschaften*), burghers conducted their political affairs largely through face-to-face exchange. Up to at least the seventeenth century, man-media like speech, body, ritual and performance played a much more important role than writing. Script – and eventually print – were used for representational and archival purposes, i.e. in merely supporting roles. A fundamental restructuring of political communication only occurred through the routinized procedures of territorial bureaucracies and the emergence of a more abstract public sphere based on distance-media like newspapers and periodicals [103 and 104: 'Introductions']. Closer examination of media use in late medieval English parishes (cf. Chapter 3), however, suggests that this dichotomy between

Figure 4 Communal life was punctuated by ceremonies and rituals. Civic processions, which re-negotiated – rather than just reflected – political power, formed particular highlights. This busy scene, captured on the day when the newly elected Lord Mayor of London travelled upstream to swear allegiance to the crown, features the barges of the city (centre-right), several livery companies and a multitude of other participants. As a Venetian, the artist knew all about urban pageantry. Antonio Canaletto, 'Westminster Bridge from the North with the Lord Mayor's Procession, 29 October 1746' (oil on canvas, 95.9 × 127.6 cm). Yale Center for British

'advanced' central and 'traditional' local political life may be too stark and that we should not underestimate the growing complexity and differentiation of communication structures in pre-modern towns and villages. In the Swiss Confederation, too, the consolidation of local government, pursuit of territorial expansion and the need for political co-ordination – through the diplomatic platform of the Diet – led to a complex combination of oral and written exchange from the late Middle Ages and, subsequently, periodic reorganization of archives to improve the accessibility of information. Here we can see how the use of texts started to restructure communication, for instance by prompting readers to respond or take certain actions, rather than merely to record it [247; 251; cf. 295]. By this point, as even more strikingly demonstrated by the global powers of the Dutch and Venetian republics, communal communication cultures had progressed much beyond the type of face-to-face exchange idealized in Aristotle's Greek *polis*.

The significance of the 'new' cultural history for our purposes is manifold. Over and beyond the acknowledgment of self-representation through civic buildings, public art (especially the symbolically charged fresco cycles in Renaissance town halls), and public rituals, historians are now looking to decipher the intricate interweaving of oral, manuscript and printed communication involving graffiti, polemical literature and libels as well as the social interaction in 'generative spaces of community' like market squares, bridges, taverns, coffee houses and apothecaries' shops [96: 10; 79]. In rural contexts, too, much of public life was played out on the interconnected stages of the parish church, public house and village hall [154: 51–3; 252: 176–8]. At East Hoathly in rural East Sussex, for example, the shopkeeper and diarist Thomas Turner regularly conducted communal business at the Crown alehouse run by John Jones. On 26 December 1755, the occasion was 'a meeting of the parish for choosing of surveyors', on 18 March 1756 'a public vestry for the making [of] a poor book' (where unfortunately 'some or most of them being a little in liquour, they could not agree'), while on 19 April he joined fellow officials for a dinner of 'a buttock of beef and ham, and plum pudding and greens' at 12 d a head [17: 19, 35, 38].

A good illustration of the vibrancy – and at times hegemonistic ambitions – of this field is a set of case studies 'reconsidering' political culture in the Holy Roman Empire: shifts in decision-making, local memory and media systems are all scrutinized for their wider implications, often with recourse to Niklas Luhmann's 'social systems theory'. His seminal work aimed to explain societies through a philosophical and sociological analysis of prevailing communication structures. At post-Reformation Cologne and Lübeck, for example, the rise of writing 'increased the communicative distance between authorities and civic corporations' to the extent that communal assemblies became mere platforms for the ceremonial promulgation of norms, while the growth in formal petitioning – tapping into the sovereign privilege of granting grace – helped Esslingen's councillors to 'extend their symbolic capital' [Hoffmann-Rehnitz and Schlaak in 241: 23, 42]. Given the vulnerability of public order, authorities sought to defuse delicate moments like elections through carefully orchestrated proceedings, ideally within a religious framework, but disruptions by contingencies, challenges and new variables could never be ruled out. A case in point is the transformative effect of mass media like printed pamphlets, which dramatically extended the range of agents affecting urban crises like the Fettmilch rising at Frankfurt in the 1610s [Würgler in 104].

This expansion of research questions and methodical tools is surely welcome, but the new cultural history should not lose touch with the norms, structures and socio-economic conditions of the local communities it investigates. As with many previous 'turns', there are dangers in prioritizing one set of fashionable approaches over others. Pre-modern polities manifested themselves as much in 'concrete' taxes, boundaries and military actions as 'symbolic' representations [254: 143–4].

Summary

To conclude this chapter with a brief recapitulation of key findings, the first important observation is the fact that communal organization 'was never static' [152: 222]. The main units of towns, villages and parishes emerged shortly after the first millennium and developed a remarkable dynamic in the late Middle Ages, assisted in part by the relatively favourable socio-economic conditions for the third estate after the Black Death. Drawing on distinct values such as the right to a livelihood, the pursuit of the common good, the rule of customary law and the ideal of personal freedom, communal government relied on principles like elections, limited terms of office and the accountability of all representatives. The general process of communalization extended to the ecclesiastical sphere, where burghers and villagers enhanced lay control to ensure access to the sacraments, value for money and – ideally – the right to appoint the parson. While collective worship, brotherly love, voluntary association, broad participation and the need for co-ordination strengthened inner bonds, kinship allegiances, social differences, gender inequalities and political factions represented centrifugal forces in operation at the same time. There was thus no linear evolution from an original, cohesive age of 'community' towards a modern, more atomized 'society' [65b], but a continuous negotiation of these contrasting factors. Communal resources ranged from common land and public buildings to local rates and voluntary donations, with overall levels varying dramatically depending on territory and socio-economic context. Communication cultures rested above all on face-to-face interaction, even though script and print made considerable inroads from the late Middle Ages, by no means just for supporting or archival purposes. In some urban and parochial contexts, media systems became differentiated and comparatively 'advanced' well before the Age of Enlightenment.

Following this 'internal' survey, it is now time to broaden the perspective to 'external relations', i.e. the manifold ways in which local communities were embedded in – and interacted with – other units of social, political and ecclesiastical organization at the local, regional and (supra-)territorial levels.

5 Interactions

Towns, villages and parishes entered into relationships with a wide range of other agents and institutions. Some existed within their own boundaries, others had focal points well beyond their sphere of influence; some interactions were voluntary and conducted in an essentially harmonious manner, others derived from external pressure with the potential to cause considerable tensions. This chapter surveys an illustrative spectrum of evidence to highlight the multilayered embedding of local communities at *any* point in time [126], and the long-term intensification of exchange with the powers of Church and state in particular. It starts with a look at local and regional settings; proceeds to contacts with secular and ecclesiastical lords; and concludes with an assessment of the growing interaction with central bodies.

Local and regional landscapes

Given the dynamic evolution of communities observed above, it is not always easy to demarcate their precise extent, to differentiate them from other local associations and to assess their place within people's loyalty networks. First, different types of local communities could co-exist and overlap. Urban householders, for example, were always simultaneously parishioners. Occasionally the respective boundaries coincided, but more often there were either several different parishes within the same town (an extreme case is London with over 100) or urban parishes extended into the surrounding countryside (as at Ashburton in Devon), thus incorporating or intersecting with secular units like vills and manors. In such cases, as has been observed for south-western Germany, ecclesiastical links could have integrative effects: through regular visits, financial investment, burial sites or election into parochial offices, rural parishioners of a town church might develop strong ties to the respective burghers, as well as an awareness of greater urban freedom. At Memmingen in Upper Swabia, freeholders from the surrounding area voluntarily subjected themselves and their holdings to the high altar of the parish church and thus, effectively, to the town council as its legal protector [162]. In a more proactive manner, late medieval towns enhanced their influence over hinterlands by means of political affiliation. A principal tool was the granting of civic rights to select individuals and groups (known as *Aus-* or *Pfalburger* in German-speaking regions), typically members of the gentry seeking an urban power base or peasants looking for a way out of feudal subordination. Added to the strategies of military conquests, acquisition of scattered jurisdictional powers and purchase of manorial rights practised by all ambitious city states, these expansive moves – viewed with open hostility by local nobles and princes – turned many landscapes into patchworks of rivalling spheres of influence rather than neatly demarcated polities. Depending on the local topography of ecclesiastical and secular rights over persons, lands and spiritualities, one and the same household could find itself within a number of different systems and orbits. What exactly was meant by 'Florence' or 'Nuremberg' thus varied by situation and perspective [135].

While separate communal affiliations need to be distinguished for analytical purposes, members at the time probably changed hats quite easily, depending on the specific context and objectives. Parishes formed the most universal units in England, but urban congregations simultaneously had a chance to participate in an expanding network of 'city commonwealths' governed by the 'civic and civil values' of middling sort freemen [115: 266–7]. As we have seen with respect to community formation, there were particularly strong overlaps and interactions between village and parish communities [193: 31]. At Gersau on Lake Lucerne, charters – referring to exactly the same target group – sometimes used the ecclesiastical term 'parishioners' [*Kilchgenossen*], but on other occasions the more secular 'people of the land' [*Landleute*; 12: Charters, nos 9, 43]. Medieval English peasants, officially under the feudal jurisdiction of a manor court, found ways to establish informal village assemblies with a degree of legislative capacity. Underlining their three-dimensional existence, many of these by-laws assigned fines for infringements neither to manorial nor village coffers, but to the fabric funds of the local parish church [117]. Some religious fraternities, in turn, had very close ties to parishes; those dedicated to the *Saint-Esprit* in southern France comprised nearly all householders, blurring the line between territorial organization and voluntary association. Following the Reformation-induced dissolution of 'superstitious' guilds in England after 1547, towns and parishes tried their best to minimize the loss of – what were in their view – communal resources. Contrary to the intentions of parliamentary statutes, which assigned all of the respective property to the crown, local communities appropriated a considerable proportion by arguing – not always entirely convincingly – that benefactors had originally bequeathed these lands for the educational and financial support of their localities rather than the enhancement of prayers for the dead [Farnhill in 175]. Fewer synergies existed where fraternities transcended local boundaries. At Ludlow in Shropshire until the Reformation era, the Palmers' Guild linked prominent inhabitants of St Laurence with social elites from all over England, potentially eroding parochial loyalties and enhancing the degree of external influence [184: 151].

It was perhaps a natural step to proceed from local collaboration to regional association. As in many other respects, northern Italian cities set the pace, famously winning recognition of extensive privileges from Emperor Barbarossa in 1183 after joining forces in the Lombard League (see Chapter 1). In the Central Alps, from the late thirteenth century, the valleys of Uri, Schwyz and Unterwalden linked up in a series of treaties aimed at preserving the peace and securing mutual assistance in times of threat. As they swore in the oldest preserved document of 1291:

> In the name of God, Amen. It is an honourable deed and conducive to the common good, when treaties, which serve the cause of peace and calm, are preserved in a proper fashion ... May everyone hear that, considering the dangerous times and the better defence and preservation of their goods, the men of the valley of Uri, the commune of the valley of Schwyz and all those of Unterwalden ... have pledged in good faith to assist each other with help, good advice and furtherance, with their bodies and belongings, within their valleys and beyond, with all power and might, against any collective body or individuals attacking

one or all of them, disturbing them, committing injustices and show-ing evil intent against them and their property. And each commune has promised to come to the aid of the others in all cases of need, at their own cost and to the extent necessary, to resist evil attacks and to redress any injustice [291].

This agreement of mutual aid – without interference in each other's internal affairs – not only stood the test of time for the three forest cantons involved, who have remained linked ever since, but also appealed to neighbouring towns. The first city to join was Lucerne in 1332 and what started as a response to a particular set of regional problems eventually evolved into the Swiss Confederation [225: 20, 184; 268 somewhat implausibly re-interprets the 1291 source as an aristocratic fabrication]. On the latter's eastern and southern bor-ders, furthermore, similar unions emerged in the Alpine valleys of the Valais and the Grisons, where communal associations – *Zenden* and *Bünde* with an explicitly 'democratic' constitution – stripped the local bishops of Sion and Chur of any secular powers in the course of the Reformation and became associates [*zugewandte Orte*] of the Swiss [217; 147].

The longevity of such urban/rural combinations is highly unu-sual, but we know of dozens of shorter-term leagues formed in the Holy Roman Empire from the late Middle Ages, sometimes – as in the case of the Swabian League founded in 1488 – linking burgh-ers even to nobles, prelates and princes. A particularly remark-able experiment took place on the Empire's northern periphery in present-day Schleswig-Holstein. Benefitting from a remote geo-graphical setting on the North Sea coast and the relative weak-ness of their feudal lord, the Archbishop of Bremen, a number of parishes gradually acquired political power of their own. By the mid-fifteenth century, they had joined forces to establish the peas-ant republic of Dithmarschen, built on a range of shared institu-tions like the assembly, a governing body known as the Forty-Eight and the codified land law of 1447. This communally-based polity survived strong external pressure up until a military defeat by the King of Denmark and the Duke of Holstein in 1559, but retained a degree of autonomy even after its eventual subjection under princely rule [204].

Apart from deliberate political associations, communities found themselves in other forms of regional embedding. From a socio-economic perspective, the 'central-place' theory of the German geographer Walter Christaller has proved particularly influential. Assuming a homogenous commercial space, he devised a system in which smaller localities arranged themselves around a central town in a geometrical pattern composed of regular hexagons, with ideal positions on the periphery varying in line with functions such as market distribution, traffic flows and administrative convenience. While stimulating in many respects, and backed up with empirical evidence in certain contexts, the model has met with a mixed reception among historians [for a comparative evaluation, with recourse to related 'landscape' and 'network' concepts, see 82b]. In a review of the victualling networks in early modern Europe, for example, Anne Radeff found a much more complex combination of centralities and decentralities, for instance, evidence for small traders who dispensed with the mediating services of urban merchants and regional centres in favour of advertising and transporting their goods directly to far-away metropolitan markets; some travelling for months from provincial France to fairs in northern Italy. This reinforces a growing consensus that the bulk of trading activity in pre-industrial Europe cannot be pressed into a rigid commercial hierarchy [262].

Yet local communities should never be viewed in isolation. As has been demonstrated for the south-west of the Holy Roman Empire from the 1520s, burghers and councils actively sought the advice of other towns and cities when faced with crucial decisions. Mutual support and the exchange of resources, especially preachers, proved vital for the spread of the evangelical faith, with reforming centres like Nuremberg and Augsburg playing particularly important parts in the political constellations of such urban landscapes [76]. The manifold ties between towns and surrounding rural communities have already been mentioned. In the middle of the last century, Hektor Ammann proposed a three-tiered concept of urban influence: strongest in the immediate surroundings, considerable within a zone extending over one or two days' travel and still perceptible up to about one hundred kilometres. As illustrated for late medieval Basel by means of an ingenious analysis of subscribers to a city lottery and the notebook of a powerful merchant, the city's centripetal force was indeed striking within a 30-kilometre radius. Commercial dependencies, credit relationships and cultural dominance, however, were two-edged swords, fostering affinities as well as tensions, and Basel never held a monopoly over the lives and outlooks of people in its immediate region [60]. It is now more generally accepted among urban historians that towns were not the sole engines of socio-economic and cultural development in pre-modern Europe. City–country relations varied dramatically between regions, depending on factors like dependent territories, guild privileges, proto-industrialization and the degree of agrarian commercialization. Overall, the picture is one of 'functional specialisation and division of labour within growing markets', with an area's profile mainly affected by institutional frameworks like 'the extent of urban jurisdictional coercion' and state intervention through market regulation and taxation [48: 8, 13].

Reviewing the evidence so far, we have seen much mutual reinforcement, economic exchange and complementary activity between towns, villages, parishes and other units of local association. Yet it would be misleading to assume that comparable structures, social backgrounds and values necessarily fostered friendly relations. There were very real conflicts about territory, resources and power. Neighbouring cities clashed over regional pre-eminence – as exemplified by the fierce rivalry of Florence and Siena in medieval Tuscany; parishes sued chapel communities over customary payments to the mother church – as in numerous disputes heard in English diocesan courts; Alpine villages like Gersau and Vitznau fell out over access to common lands on their boundaries [7: 630] and – fuelled by the religious divisions of the confessional age – tensions between the Swiss cantons repeatedly escalated into military confrontation. Zurich's Reformed leader Huldrych Zwingli famously died on the battlefield of Kappel in October 1531, where his corpse was ritually humiliated, quartered and burnt by the troops of fellow Catholic confederates [245a: 133]. Just as we have seen with regard to internal relations in Chapter 4, an overall assessment has to acknowledge incidences of affinity and collaboration alongside frequent tensions. The history of inter-communal relations is one of occasional, conditional or 'ambiguous' harmony, in which burghers, villagers and parishioners weighed up a series of conflicting considerations – ranging from coarse self-interest via neighbourly solidarity to diplomatic obligations – before embarking on a course of action in each and every case.

Local communities and their lords

An even greater ambivalence characterized communal relationships with feudal lords. Looking through the sources, ranging
from grants of agricultural holdings via manorial accounts to
court records, we find the whole spectrum of possible relations:
from amicable to neutral and irreparably damaged, with situ-
ational combinations of deference and confrontation. Customary
sets of dues and services had to be offered every quarter or year,
usually with little sign of open dissent, but new obligations were
never popular and changes of ownership another potential cause
of friction. It is virtually impossible to arrive at unambiguous conclusions, given the infinite variety of specific legal and chronological contexts, not least because of the fact that communities
could hold feudal prerogatives themselves. In medieval Italy, *stati
cittadini* (civic states) exercised very direct power over their *contado*,
i.e. the sort of 'urban jurisdictional coercion' mentioned above.
Like princes elsewhere, city councils acted as territorial rulers with
rights of high jurisdiction, taxation and legislation. Equally like
feudal lords, they insisted on the prompt payment of contributions
and dues, often with a clear target to increase rather than ease
the overall burden on rural subjects. Similar, if less compact, city-
states can be found in the Holy Roman Empire, but not in countries like France, Spain or England, where the central monarchy
and nobility remained strong enough to monopolize these powers
[74: 155–8].

One major trend, perhaps, is the relative improvement of fortunes
for members of local communities after the heavy population losses
of the Black Death in the mid-fourteenth century. In many of the
regional contexts examined in this book, notably England, terms
of tenure became more favourable and serfdom effectively extinct
[249]. Yet the traditional dichotomy between a 'freer', manorial west
of Europe, where rural householders produced fairly independently
and with scope for market involvement, and an 'enserfed' east, where
peasants were personally tied to the vast demesnes of grain-export-
ing estates, looks much less absolute in the light of recent research.
In-depth examination of conditions both east and west of the river
Elbe, the usual dividing line, reveals a complex pattern of highly differentiated forms of agricultural systems. It was perfectly possible to
end up with signs of servility – such as restricted mobility, limited

marriage partners and political marginalization – in the German south-west, while there is evidence for relatively benign regimes, inclusive of considerable village autonomy, under some Junkers in Brandenburg-Prussia [272; 134; cf. Chapter 2]. Most of early modern Europe, furthermore, faced similar socio-economic problems caused by demographic pressures from the early sixteenth century. In a reversal of the late medieval 'golden age', land became scarce, competition for holdings increased, property tended to concentrate in the hands of rural elites and the proportion of landless labourers – with the associated need for welfare provision – increased.

Even though the level of urbanization remained dramatically higher in central and north-western Europe than in the east, the relevance of non-feudal, civic dimensions extended far beyond the communal heartlands, particularly into the Commonwealth of Poland-Lithuania, and – with further limitations – places like the Hanseatic outpost of Novgorod in Muscovy [216]. Russia, of course, is rightly known for autocratic rule, feudal resilience and almost-universal peasant serfdom. Yet even here scholars find traces of communal structures, albeit under tight seigneurial direction. In some regions and contexts, especially where lords were absentees and obligations restricted to monetary payments, the village commune [*mir*] exercised a range of local government functions, allocated corporate liabilities, periodically re-distributed holdings, exercised petty jurisdiction and initiated changes like the introduction of new crops: these communities thus 'played a very large role in administering rural Russia throughout the period ... and were at the interface of the peasant world and the world of the landowning and ruling elites'. The endowment and maintenance of local churches provided yet more scope for comparable initiatives, albeit as a consequence of pragmatic responses to real problems rather than a 'natural, Slavic' propensity to collective action [140: 228; Stefanovich in 136].

Another general characteristic of external seigneurial relations is communal resilience. Lords could not simply ride roughshod over local customs and rights. The case studies of Part 1 have highlighted corporate memory and extensive record-keeping as important safeguards, but – according to Peter Blickle – communal organization posed a much more fundamental threat to feudalism in pre-modern Europe. The principle of horizontal ties among equals was diametrically opposed to the vertical subordination of commoners under nobles; the ideal of the common good incompatible with the demand of fealty to an individual. Given the balance of power in most contexts, communalism had to co-exist with feudal structures, but almost like a 'fifth column' with a latent potential to undermine them from within. This is an aspect of a larger debate we will have to come back to in Part III [42: Vol. ii, 374–9].

Relations with ecclesiastical bodies were in many ways comparable to those with secular lords, as countless manors had accrued to the 'dead hand' of the Church over the course of the Middle Ages. Religious houses, diocesan authorities and colleges used their estates to generate economic and personal resources just like other landholders. Regardless of their Christian credentials, prelates could treat tenants very harshly – often in fact in exploitative forms of serfdom. Their combined spiritual-material power was an important cause of anticlerical feeling and a major factor in the special targeting of religious institutions during the German Peasants' War of 1524–26, especially where they had also appropriated large portions of parochial tithes [240]. Yet there were two further, related points of friction: pastoral visitations and the operation of ecclesiastical courts. Throughout Europe in theory, but with considerable regional variation in diocesan practice, bishops and/or archdeacons were expected to tour their areas of spiritual jurisdiction at regular intervals. Equipped with a pre-formulated set of questions – usually focused on the performance of the clergy, the religious beliefs of the laity, the moral behaviour of all inhabitants, the conduct of services and the maintenance of church buildings – external dignitaries came to towns and villages in a decidedly inquisitive spirit. For parishioners, this could be a welcome opportunity to present heretics, dissolute householders and negligent parsons for censure, but the process also involved less popular elements like clampdowns on festive traditions, prohibitions of unsanctioned local cults and the enforcement of the full range of ecclesiastical dues [see the particularly detailed documentation in 31]. Proceedings, furthermore, could be long and costly, with – as in the diocese of Strasbourg on the eve of the Reformation – blatant abuses such as random citations of innocent individuals, the extraction of extortionate fees and the excessive use of heavy penalties like excommunications. This was by no means the norm, and many visitors conducted their business in a constructive and sympathetic fashion, but there was always scope for a 'clash of cultures'. As evident from post-Reformation examples in Lutheran, Reformed as well as Catholic contexts, tensions intensified further when Church and – increasingly – secular authorities used visitations and courts to enforce new confessional regimes and enhanced standards of social discipline. It was quite possible that the process left both communities ruffled and central officials frustrated [201; 27a; 21].

On the more positive side, western European local communities appear as remarkably committed Christians. Dissenters and unorthodox beliefs can always be found, of course, but on the whole burghers and peasants allocated a considerable part of their disposable resources into mainstream observances, especially those based in their parishes (Chapter 3). Anticlerical feelings tended to relate to individuals and specific concerns, while clergymen in general – as God's servants – were treated with respect. Few Protestants doubted that minsters were necessary for religious instruction and few Catholics disputed the sacramental role of priests. We have already observed how the 'reciprocal' doctrine of Purgatory and corporate parish worship mutually reinforced each other in late medieval Catholicism. Evangelical German peasant rebels, in turn, actively sought the advice of theologians – like the Zwinglian preacher Christoph Schappeler at Memmingen – when drawing up their demands for greater communal powers over clerical appointments, ecclesiastical property and agricultural resources, even though their main hope and source of inspiration, Martin Luther, soon distanced himself from their seamless integration of the sacred and secular spheres [16: 251–76]. A little earlier, however, Luther had approved an entirely parish-based organization of local religion. In a preface to a set of practical guidelines for 'all Christians of the commune of Leisnig' in 1523, he even recommended it as an example for all others to follow. This ordinance, a 'brotherly union' drawn up by 'the honourable men, councillors, neighbourhood masters, elders and common inhabitants of the town as well as surrounding villages ... of the parish of Leisnig', stipulated in particular:

> We will and shall use ... our Christian freedom, as relating to the appointment of our common parson (including his invitation, election, institution and dismissal to our cure of souls, aimed solely at the preaching of the word of god and the administration of sacraments), in no other way than according to the explanation and ordinances of ... the biblical scriptures ...

We will and shall, as far as God's grace allows, faithfully hear ... the salutary and comforting word of God ... for our improvement, at the appointed days and hours, which applies to all male and female householders, for themselves as well as their children and servants ...
[In the interests of] brotherly love and ... gentle works of mercy, ... the parish assembly ... has set up a common chest [containing all assets and revenues of both the benefice and fabric of the church. Each year] the common parish assembly, meeting at the town hall, shall consensually elect, from amongst all of them, with sole regard to their virtue ... ten wardens or proctors for the common chest; namely, two honourable patricians, two of the ruling council, three from among the common burghers and three from among the peasants in the country ...
This common chest and container shall be stored in the safest place of our church and secured with four separate locks and keys, so that one can be kept by the patricians, one by the council, one by the urban parishioners and one by the peasants ...
For the common good of our parish assembly, the ten wardens ... shall use the common chest to buy ... a fair sum and amount of corn and peas to keep in stock ...
Each year, all of our ten wardens shall deliver ... their complete annual accounts, detailing assets, income and expenses of our common chest ... publicly and in the presence of our common assembly ... [27b: 6–24].

Parish life and organization clearly had a massive influence on the overall shape of religious movements. There was no inherent affinity between local communities and *any* of the mainstream confessions, since all of the 'territorial' Churches – as opposed to selective sects – could be 'communalized' to a remarkable extent (see Chapter 6). Religious preference depended on a complex combination of individual, collective and external factors, although higher authorities usually had the decisive say. In the few cases where commoners were asked to express a preference, the result could go either way, even in comparable socio-political contexts: 'Reformed' at Zurich in 1523, 'Catholic' at Solothurn 1529 [61: 279; 245a: 57–61, 121].

In this sense, the study of communal society reinforces two wider historiographical trends: the relativization of the Reformation(s) as a turning-point in European history on the one hand, and the detection of 'functional similarities' between the principal early modern confessions on the other. Sixteenth-century transformations now tend to be embedded in a longer reform process initiated in the late

Middle Ages, while – in the seminal concept of 'confessionalization' – features like the clarification of doctrine, improvements in religious education and greater emphasis on social discipline are associated with early modern Catholicism, Lutheranism and Calvinism alike [201; 269; 248]. As in many other fields, however, it would be wrong to press revisionism too far. It is true that the Communal Age neither started nor ended in the Reformation period and it is equally true that losses in one section (parish endowments) could be compensated by gains in another (many English towns bolstered their corporate resources and infrastructure thanks to the acquisition of former church land: [110]). In areas like the Grisons and the Valais, furthermore, the weakening of prelate power proved essential for the full development of communal potential. Yet we have seen how traumatic religious change could be at grass-roots level, where families and entire communities found themselves divided and sucked into decades of conflict and persecution, sometimes outright war (not least in the Grisons [Head in 136]); where close spiritual bonds with ancestors and benefactors were cut almost overnight; and where iconoclasm, campaigns for moral regeneration, redefinition of gender roles and new forms of representation altered communal cultures in dramatic ways. The Reformation may not have been the absolute watershed of traditional scholarship, but it sparked an incisive chain of change and adaptation for local communities in 'confessional' Europe [94; 24; 128; 157; 170; 76].

Surveying communal preferences over the *longue durée*, a combination of well-equipped churches, commemoration of ancestors, preaching of the Gospel, diligent clergy, veneration of Biblical saints (especially Mary, the archetypal model of virtue and compassion), emphasis on the passion of Christ, general respect for divine law, lay control over resources, support of the deserving poor and scope for neighbourly sociability would have won a genuinely 'free vote' in most pre-modern parishes, but in reality nobody offered such a programme.

Relations with central authorities

The single biggest process affecting external relations in *all* contexts was the rise of the state. As the ninth of the Twelve Articles drawn up by the Swabian peasants in 1525 complained, 'we are burdened with a great evil in the constant making of new laws. ... In our opinion we should be judged according to the old written law so that the case shall be decided according to its merits' [16: 252–7]. Frequent legislation and recourse to learned, Roman law were indeed two prominent aspects of state building. Starting in the fifteenth century, princes – alongside city-states – endeavoured to remove rivalling powers, to harmonize the constitutional framework and to tighten their control throughout their lands. From the mid-1500s, they also encroached on previously ecclesiastical spheres of influence, chiefly church administration, moral supervision, systems of poor relief and education. The 'well-ordered police state' sought greater central powers to improve subjects' lives from above, greater military capacity to enhance dynastic prestige, greater bureaucracy to manage increasing responsibilities and greater taxation to finance all of these complex tasks [263; 234]. Local communities were very directly affected. More and more aspects of everyday life, from the wearing of clothes to the prevention of fires, attracted uniform regulation across an entire polity, backed up by an enforcement machinery involving regional officials, periodic visitations, surveys, central courts and, if need be, armed force. On the whole, throughout central and western Europe, we can observe either a more or less extensive state appropriation of existing local government structure – as in the case of the English parish – or the establishment of a new hierarchy of central officials – as exemplified by the French *intendants*. For many historians of local communities, this smacked of 'defeat' [92: Pt 1].

There can be no doubt that the intensity of centre–periphery contacts increased and that towns, villages and parishes operated in a more integrated political culture in the early modern period (see Figure 5). Yet the current view of state-building places a very strong emphasis on reciprocity, balancing of different interests and, above all, negotiation. Local communities were not fundamentally opposed to external power as a *subsidiary* resource, since it could help them to solve real problems and provide services which exceeded the capacity of individual towns and villages. The growth of the state could also help them to marginalize feudal powers: a combination of structural analysis – of the respective powers of communal, manorial and central institutions – and assessment of change over time in the French Dauphiné – a mountainous

Figure 5 The juxtaposition of communal and central authority in the early modern period emerges very clearly from this prospect of the Bavarian market town of Dachau. While the castle of the monarch (A) forms the biggest and most elaborate building, its position appears somewhat marginal. For the burghers, town hall (E) and parish church (B) remain the central institutions, with the latter's spire towering over the landscape and the large cemetery (H) underlining the significance of local religion. Offprint of a coloured engraving in Michael Wening, *Historico-Topographica descriptio: Das ist Beschreibung des ... Hertzogthums ... Bayrn* (pt 1, Munich, 1701), in the possession of the author.

area with strong traditions of self-government – reveals declining seigneurial influence over the course of the seventeenth century and the crucial role of local officeholder-dynasties for the growth of – predominantly fiscal – royal demands [127].

Princes and city-states more generally lacked the resources to govern all localities directly and relied on a degree of co-operation from below, often by enlisting members of communal elites who perceived state service as a possible route of social advancement [144; 157]. Far from passive objects of centralization, their 'middling sort' neighbours exercised informal influence through the compilation of *gravamina*, sets of local complaints which representative assemblies used to influence princely legislation; the formulation of petitions, presented to monarchs at personal audiences or through the appropriate administrative channels; and the remarkable readiness with which local people resorted to regional and central courts, a practice known as *Justiznutzung* [utilization of jurisdiction] or *Verrechtlichung* [juridification] in German-speaking scholarship [253]. The Swedish peasantry, in probably the most institutionalized type of bottom-up representation in early modern Europe, even had their own chamber in the Imperial Diet, while many other parliamentary assemblies – at both regional and national level – offered a formal say at least to major cities [246]. Where peaceful forms of communication broke down, early modern communities – as other subordinate groups in different regions and times – knew how to use 'weapons of the weak', the passive resistance which made government very difficult for lords as well as states [140: Ch. 7]. Then there was open, violent rebellion as a last resort. Active resistance did not cease in early modern Europe, not even after the crushing defeat of the German Peasants War. Here, again, local communities appear among the main carriers and organizational frameworks. Most risings failed, but some achieved indirect improvements and others revealed the multiple fault lines which continued to haunt early modern states [274; 233; 78: 192; 138].

Summary

Reviewing the nature of local/regional and central power relations, we should thus not overstate the transformations around 1500.

Multiple forms of interaction between local communities persisted across this traditional watershed and 'parochial' interests / agents continued to play an important role in early modern public life, while attempts to increase pressure from the centre could have centripetal as well as centrifugal effects: a streamlined body of subjects in some places, a reinforcement of existing divisions and tensions elsewhere [52: 84–5]. The titles of many recent works – 'local communities *and* the state in old Europe', 'state building as a cultural process' and 'empowering interactions' – convey the emerging consensus of sustained exchange between princes and subjects, albeit in a partnership of distinctly unequal power [41; 228; 235]. Historians are now inclined 'to interpret the dynamics of power as a many-sided and multi-layered communication in which ordinary people were active participants, sometimes in confrontation with the state and the privileged orders, sometimes as donors of legitimacy, and always as arbiters of effective governance in everyday life'. Within towns, villages and parishes themselves, furthermore, 'communal values ... still governed popular politics' in the eighteenth century, as they had for generations before [255: 480, 489; cf. 186].

PART III Assessment

In this final section, the emphasis shifts to historical perceptions and scholarly debates. How prominent were local communities in pre-modern minds and discourses? What did contemporaries deem worthy of analysis and critique? Which conceptualizations and theoretical reflections have emerged in more recent times? The argument concludes with a general evaluation of the significance of towns, villages and parishes in the European past.

6 Perceptions and Debates

An examination of pre-modern viewpoints can start with the community members themselves. Previous chapters have highlighted the manifold ways in which townspeople, villagers and parishioners formed and articulated specific understandings of their localities, for example through the careful preservation of acquired rights and privileges, communal crests and seals, the periodic renewal of oaths of association, collective investment in better religious provision, construction of representative buildings like town halls and the ritualized constitution of political space through elaborate processions and the periodic beating of communal bounds [110; 154: 51; Hindle in 51: 205–27]. This demonstrable sense of awareness, belonging and often pride reflected early modern horizons which were – by no means exclusively, but to a very significant extent – *local*.

Communal self-perceptions

Alongside landscapes, languages, religion, status and kinship, communal units formed the most tangible components of the matrixes in which people situated themselves. The virulence of what Italians call *campanilismo* – literally fixation on one's own bell tower – fostered a multiplicity of idiosyncratic local identities even within the same region. Towns and villages shaped these self-perceptions through their built environment, historical evolution, freedoms and political power; parishes through their ability to 'sacralize' communal structures and to facilitate an intense cult of ancestors, which expressed itself in a proliferation of memorials and a near-pervasive desire to be buried in the local churchyard [44: 156; 135: Ch. 6; 129: Ch. 2]. Spatial attributions in early modern ego-documents reinforce the

97

impression that the notion of a 'homeland' was small-scale rather than large, typically a town or parish rather than a state or nation, although people were aware of the highest overlords of kings and emperors as protectors and political figureheads. Judging from travel reports, furthermore, writers understood their journeys as point-to-point movements between specific localities, separated by precisely-known distances, rather than as movements through a sequence of abstract, three-dimensional spaces. The mental mapping of distinct polities thus resembled a cumulative assigning of individual towns and villages to particular rulers; at this stage, it seems, the crossing of physical boundaries was not yet experienced as the transition from one hermetically sealed territorial 'container' into a coterminous other [245b: 80–82, 157–8]. Early modern cartographers like Phillip Apian, who chose to depict sixteenth-century Bavaria as a landscape punctuated by small settlements with disproportionately large parish churches, underline the same point [285]. The scientific demarcation of national borders, as has recently been argued for Venice, appears to be a gradual process linked to early modern state formation and more general attempts to count, classify and fully exploit all the human and natural resources in the age of Enlightenment. Pre-modern maps of the Swiss Confederation could be remarkably vague about the precise extent of its sphere of influence, with particular allies moving in and out of focus and strong confessional variations in terms of who was deemed to be a member [89: Pt. 1; 282].

Awareness of local communities, therefore, was much sharper than that of larger units, certainly among the vast majority of the population. Physical boundary markers separated different units and the precincts of towns, villages and parish churches were secured by means of fences, walls and bastions. Early modern city maps like those produced for Amsterdam, Cologne and many others by Georg Braun and Franz Hogenberg in 1572, which featured sharp contrasts between the densely-built urban settlements and the surrounding open countryside, convey a powerful impression of communal 'distinctiveness' [287]. The message here was less about isolation, introspection and withdrawal than about assertion, i.e. the ability of towns to muster large economic and human resources. The same can be said for many rural communities: the fortified churches (*Kirchenburgen*) of the Alsace or Transylvania, for example, signalled a determination to protect the lives, possessions and rights of parishioners at a time when external raids, noble feuds and growing intensity of warfare posed very tangible threats [Fabini in 66: 306].

Throughout the Holy Roman Empire, the right to bear arms was a cherished privilege of townsmen as well as free peasants. Physical prowess and the robust defence of personal honour formed key parts of masculine identity 'and all male heads of household in early modern German cities were required to maintain weapons and to protect their town by serving on guard duty appearing armed and ready in civic emergencies'. This combination of gender norms and civic obligations fostered a pervasive 'martial ethic' in local communities [276]. Not every man was a born warrior (many of the amateur police 'forces' were in fact pretty shambolic), but the standard was high enough for Swiss troops to defeat some of the most formidable powers, particularly Charles the Bold in the Burgundian wars of the 1470s, and to become the most sought-after mercenaries in early modern armies. Even noble generals acknowledged the strength and advantages of communal military tradition. In a 1566 report on the best possible preparation for war, the imperial knight and commander Lazarus von Schwendi praised the defence customs of the Confederates and recommended the adoption of a general *Landesdefension* policy, under which all householders would be armed, local communities charged with the maintenance of shooting ranges, churches reinforced as emergency fortresses and all men mustered in their towns and villages on an annual basis [271: 187–90]. The longevity of communal organization, from its emergence within a feudal framework and throughout the challenges of economic polarization, religious division and state formation, owed much to this spirit of resilience.

Communal memory provided citizens with plentiful reasons to appreciate and defend their localities. From the earliest stages of evolution around 1100, a concerted architectural and artistic programme shaped the physical environment of cities like Pisa. Gates (*Porta Aurea*), churches (*San Sisto*) and squares (*Piazza del Duomo/dei Miracoli*) became parts of communal self-representation. Clerics and laymen, intellectuals and craftsmen all joined forces to support an image of urban achievement. With the growth of writing, epigraphy, annals and poetry provided additional means to spread the key messages of victory against the Saracens, triumph over heathens and maritime ascendancy, while glossing over the many constitutional struggles and inner-communal conflicts encountered along the way. Social coherence derived from powerful reminders of the glories of the past and explicit demarcation from the 'other' [85: 427–31; for commercial forces shaping urban space cf. 73a]. Official discourse – in town and country – focused on communal symbolism, collective liberties, the prosperity resulting from honest work, equitable government and the rule of virtues such as wisdom, prudence and learning rather than the cult of individuals and dynastic lineage as in monarchical environments. In the autonomous village of Gersau, especially, the notion of 'freedom' permeates the political language (see Figure 6).

On both sides of the Alps, we find a comparable interest in the recording and celebration of historical landmarks. The late medieval illustrated chronicles of Bern and Lucerne in the Swiss Confederation, officially endorsed by the respective city councils, provide lavish panoramas of what contemporaries considered key stages of communal development [7; 99; cf. cover illustration]. Foundation stories / myths and appeals to pursue the common good were prominent components of all works in this genre. In the small imperial free city of Schwäbisch-Gmünd, for example, the cloth merchant and mayor Paul Goldstainer urged his fellow citizens to reunite after a period of Reformation-related division. The manuscript, compiled in 1549–50 with reference to previous town histories, invoked the grace of God, the noble deeds of ancestors and – inspired by the fashionable movement of Renaissance Humanism – the model of Ancient Rome:

About the beginning and origin of the city of Gmund in Swabia.

First, as can be gathered from the old histories and chronicles, in the year one thousand, one hundred and ten after the birth of Christ, our redeemer, when the Dukes of Swabia ... ruled and preserved the Holy Roman Empire ... , the said Emperors, Kings and Dukes ... endowed Gmund with a law code, rights and liberties and placed it in the possession of the Empire as other cities in this region such as Ulm, Esslingen and Reutlingen ...

For the sake of the good works, honour, courage and example of the said princes, lords, burghers and ancestors, may all current and future officials, clerical and lay, governors and inhabitants of this imperial

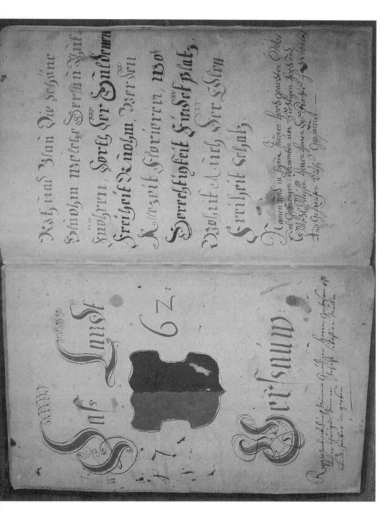

Figure 6 The title page of this collection of laws and statutes compiled by the micro-republic of Gersau in 1762 features the colours of the communal crest, circumscribed by the phrase 'The Land of Gersau', on the left, and the following inscription on the right: 'Red and blue, the beautiful flower which Gersau carries, there the fame of golden freedom will always flourish; as where justice reigns, the treasure of noble freedom also shines'. District Archive of Gersau, LB 4: Landbuch no. 4, inside cover. Photo: Beat Kümin. Reproduced by kind permission of the District Archive / District Council of Gersau.

free city of Gmund observe the town's common good, not letting anything prevent it, so that the city can be governed and preserved in the
best civic, peaceful love and unity. As Cicero, the famous orator of the
Roman Senate, said: among all the communes and societies, there
is no firmer and superior one than that [guided by] an assembly of
good, pious men of equal good morals ... Yet [despite the city's imperial
descent and noble ancestry], so much disagreement and discord has
arisen among the various families, that they resent each other's good
fortune, honour and prosperity as granted by God the Allmighty ... May
He bestow his grace and immeasurable mercy on the council and all
inhabitants of this laudable city of Gmund to enable a happy government full of prosperity, peace and civic unity, so that we may enjoy the
joy of eternal salvation ... after this temporary life. May we be granted
this by God the father, son and the holy ghost. Amen [289: 239–42].

In the confessional age, the writing of chronicles acquired a fresh
urgency to forge and proclaim new city identities and distinguish
them from others, especially those of a different faith. Closer study
of examples from northern Germany underlines their versatility
as educational, moralizing and religious tools, offering present-
day historians unrivalled insights into communal self-perceptions,
the instrumentalization of the past for political purposes and the
early development of their own academic discipline. The chronicles'
potential to illuminate early modern urban society on the one hand,
and the evolution of historiographical techniques on the other, has
also been emphasized for eighteenth-century England [101; 109].

We have already seen that intensive engagement with the evolution of local communities was not just an urban phenomenon.
Facilitated by growing literacy rates, rural areas also reflected
on the history and present state of their villages and leagues [cf.
Chapter 2; 217]. Some writers did this for purely personal motives,
adding notes to diaries and autobiographies, others acted in an
official capacity and with a deliberate intent of tradition to future
generations. One example of the former is the chronicle of the
Hessian village of Strausebach by the prosperous peasant Caspar
Preis. Covering the traumatic period of the Thirty Years War, it
provides fascinating glimpses into the consequences of military
conflict and local attempts to preserve a semblance of normality:

[*Entry for 1645:*] Dear, oh dear, how terrible and miserable were conditions during the year 1645 in these parts ...

[*Entry for 1649–50:*] We at Strausebach ... have had to do without a priest for 4 years ... Yet, since thanks to God we have such a beautiful church, we agreed to continue to frequent it and to worship God at least a little. Each Sunday and feast day we resorted there. We rang the bells in the morning, as if a priest were in attendance. [Following a hymn,] I, poor Caspar, took the book, read from the Gospel and made a sermon. Then we knelt down and prayed, sang again and returned home [15: 58, 70].

At the same time, in the rural territory of Bern, a conservative villager kept a similar record. Jost von Brechershäusern, who lived in a small hamlet near the Emmental, deplored the loosening morals in his community, where 'unnecessarily expensive weddings and superfluous feasts' apparently caused greater problems than elsewhere, and the civil strife within the Swiss Confederation. Having assembled a large fortune, he showed little sympathy for the armed rising of the Peasants War of 1653, denouncing the rebellion as a 'damnable rising against our gracious lords'. His chronicle, which covered local as well as (supra-)regional affairs, was written 'during long nights, without wasting any working time, and solely for my entertainment', in the hope of recording for his offspring 'what I have seen myself' [9: 97, 105, 95].

A more formal custom in some areas was the storage of local chronicles, together with other documents and valuables, in the *Turmkugeln* (tower capsules) of parish church spires. In a remarkable case of periodic and corporate stock-taking, usually during major repairs, local communities produced records of important village events and historical facts for the instruction of future generations, who would add to the capsules' collections on subsequent occasions in turn. We have come across this for Gersau, but similar early modern practices are documented for other parishes in Central Switzerland, Bavaria, Saxony and beyond. Contents included information on village rights, officials and building projects, but also records of natural disasters, prices of commodities, communal devotions, warnings against inner divisions and the occasional reference to the wider historical context – another source type which merits much closer investigation. The first preserved example from Gersau, written by the official scribe Anton Nigg on 24 September 1655, contained the following passage:

At the point when this letter will be opened by our descendants, may they ask God Almighty to forgive the sins and misdeeds of us, the present inhabitants, and the benefactors of our church with a general Christian prayer. May this land also be graciously preserved in the true Catholic faith, in its ancient God-given liberties, obtained by our ancestors from the old Emperors and kings and faithfully handed down to us, and may it always be consensually governed in good peace and prosperity, for what discord can cause in our land we have had to experience to our greatest disadvantage [a reference to an acrimonious constitutional conflict fought over the exclusion of a local family from citizenship during the preceding decades; 30: 168].

Communal culture and pre-modern thought

Moving outside the localities themselves, numerous learned discourses engaged with communal organization directly or indirectly. Complementing the default assumption that *ideas* shape real-life policy, as exemplified by the German historicist school or the indebtedness of communist regimes to the writings of Karl Marx, recent research has stressed that the theories of many thinkers were heavily influenced by communal *practice*. In his *Discorsi* on political matters, Niccolò Machiavelli extolled the merits, unity and strict equality of the Swiss republics, holding up their uncorrupted religious devotion, military valour and self-government as a model for the spoilt and faction-prone feudal lords of his native land [Kapossy in 227: 229–30]. In many instances, of course, the exact nature of (cross-)fertilization remains hidden to the modern observer, but it is certainly notable that leading late medieval lawyers like Baldus de Ubaldis studied and taught in Italian cities, that Humanist reformers like Martin Bucer and Huldrych Zwingli hailed from heavily communalized backgrounds in the Alsace and Swiss Toggenburg respectively and that a seminal Enlightenment philosopher like Jean-Jacques Rousseau was born in the urban republic of Geneva.

The basic principles of communal organization did not need to be invented by anyone. There were historical precedents and parallels in Ancient Greek philosophy, notably Aristotle's *polis*, the Roman Republic and the constitutional practices of medieval church councils [231]. Yet after the first millennium, the expansion to the rural world and the sheer proliferation of villages and parishes throughout the Continent propelled the phenomenon to a new level. In a series of works published over the last three decades,

Peter Blickle has offered the most detailed analyses of the ways in which the communal principle interacted with the theology, legal theory and political thought of the late medieval and early modern periods [see 212, 42, 232 and esp. 43: 24–8]. This is highly complex and contested ground, requiring a degree of engagement with specialist discourses which goes beyond the parameters of a short survey. Yet, in an attempt to provide some basic impressions, the main lines of argument will be outlined here.

In the religious sphere, Blickle detected a close affinity between the socio-political ideals of villages and towns on the one hand, and the message of the Protestant reformers on the other. Following strenuous moves to communalize the Church in the late Middle Ages, a campaign credited with an important part in the Christianization of Europe, the laity responded with enthusiasm to Luther's early emphasis on congregational powers at the expense of clerical prerogatives (cf. Chapter 5). The prospect of hearing God's 'pure Gospel' preached by a resident pastor chosen by the commune electrified peasants and burghers, who backed the fledgling movement with numerous sets of demands and ultimately violent agitation in the Peasants' War, the 'revolution of the common man' aimed at a more equitable society based on divine law [39; 40]. This concept provided a radical new interpretation of the Reformation and integrated the vast mass of the rural population into a historiography previously preoccupied with theologians, Humanists, princes and towns. At the same time, it should be noted that a communal heartland like Central Switzerland, where lay control had become very extensive well before the sixteenth century, retained the old faith, and that Catholicism, in spite of its feudal–hierarchical structure, could foster communal bonds in different ways. The doctrine of good works, the encouragement of reciprocal intercession and the (relative) tolerance of festive conviviality appear as particularly congenial elements, both before and after the Reformation. Communal control, based on independent finances and a sustained defence of lay interests, was thus not restricted to one particular confession [128; 186; 159]. Some radical Protestant denominations – especially Baptists and Independents – endowed their congregations with even more extensive powers, but aspired to a selective union of 'saints' governed by Scripture and strong moral discipline rather than associations of all householders within a given town, village or parish. Their trajectory was sectarian rather than communal.

In contemporary legal theory, a local community was classed as a *universitas*, i.e. a type of corporation with similarities to a craft formed by tradesmen, a religious house composed of monks and a university made up of scholars [56]. From the High Middle Ages, Europeans thus reflected on the significance of 'groups' formed by guilds, fraternities and neighbourhoods alongside and, at times, in tension with the vertical structuring of the society of estates [259]. According to Nicolaus Losaeus' *Tractatum de iure universitatum* of 1601, local communities were endowed with the right of legislation and governed by means of extensive consultation: in villages directly through assemblies of all members; in towns – due to higher population figures – more indirectly through elected councils. Their practices and potential became important points of reference in early modern political thought. In his seminal *Politica methodice digesta* (first edition 1603 [32]; for 3rd edition of 1614 see [284]), which followed a series of anti-tyrannical tracts written during the religious wars of Germany, France and the Netherlands, the jurist and philosopher Johannes Althusius embedded local communities into a three-tiered pyramid of consensual government. According to his model, exemplified with real-life examples from Upper Germany, independent corporations could link up with others by means of a *consociatio*, i.e. a voluntary association, first at provincial level and, in a subsequent step, stretching over the state as a whole. What mattered here, therefore, were contractual delegations of *limited* powers, quite in contrast to the *absolute* sovereignty of monarchs legitimized – according to Jean Bodin and Thomas Hobbes – by divine right and the need to prevent a ruthless clash of self-interests. In a clear reference to the history of the Swiss cantons, Althusius acknowledged that 'lower-level communities existed in their own right and could defect from the Empire' [215: 137].

In the eighteenth century, Jean-Jacques Rousseau – who was not only born in Geneva at a time of related constitutional debates, but also spent time as an exile in the Swiss canton of Bern – developed the notion of an agreed transfer of power further. In his *Contrat social* (1762; [35; 294]), infused by the Enlightenment concept of 'natural law', a truly rightful political organization emerged out of the *volonté générale* (general will) of free citizens, who were thus founders *and* subjects of the state at the same time. As in pre-modern towns, villages and parishes, all public activities had to be oriented towards the 'common good'. If necessary, this ideal could legitimize armed liberation struggles like the Dutch War of Independence and it was to become a key ideological influence on the French Revolution. While the philosopher remained sceptical about whether such a system could be realized in his own age, Blickle has no doubts that Rousseau's political theory was rooted in Europe's communal tradition [42/Vol. ii: 342–8].

Current approaches and debates

Having noted the pioneering nineteenth-century theories of Otto von Gierke and Ferdinand Tönnies in the introduction and the multiple, if rarely conjoined, historiographies of towns, villages and parishes throughout the preceding chapters, two principal concepts remain to be considered here: communalism and republicanism.

Peter Blickle developed communalism in the course of intensive engagement with the socio-political organization of burghers and peasants in the south-western part of the Holy Roman Empire [a concise English summary can be found in 40: Ch.1; the full German elaboration in 42/Vol. i]. Looking out from this base, wider geographical comparison revealed regionally diverse forms of voluntarily generated local organization in other areas of the Continent, most notably in Italian cities and Scandinavian court districts [42/Vol. ii: 374]. Ultimately, such findings informed a bold new general interpretation of 'Old Europe' between *c.* 1300 and 1800. According to this grand narrative, the fundamental building block of the household structured the Continent horizontally (in communes) as well as vertically (via noble dynasties up to the royal court); the religious models of Christ's passion and saintly martyrdom infused Europeans with a strong sense of shared suffering and compassion, i.e. a kind of 'ethic of empathy'; and the combination of neighbourly association and spiritual fervour fostered distinctive ideals like peace through law, personal freedom – for why should lords and states have the right to re-subject Christians liberated by the Lord's sacrifice? – and the well-ordered commonwealth (achieved through social disciplining and the practice of good government [232]).

Returning to our primary thematic focus, Blickle located the origins of rural communities in the transition from feudally directed demesne farming to more independent peasant agriculture, i.e. a system requiring greater local co-operation, around 1300. At the same time, town burghers associated themselves in sworn unions, meaning that analogous forms of organization emerged in city and country. Both derived from the initiative of the inhabitants themselves, making them *autokephal*/independently created; both reserved full political rights for male householders; and both gradually acquired powers of local legislation, administration and jurisdiction. Through elected representatives, the 'common man' thus exercised state functions, but – in contrast to dynastically-motivated noble rulers – with the furtherance of 'peace', 'livelihood' and the 'common good' as principal objectives. Further up the political scale, communal interests could be voiced at regional and sometimes territorial level by means of petitions, lists of grievances (*cahiers de doléance*), court proceedings and – most directly – participation in diets and other representative assemblies. By the 1520s, Reformation-inspired fervour pushed the movement towards a revolutionary climax, when commoners joined up in military bands to fight for an Empire built on communal rather than feudal foundations, the abolition of serfdom and the re-ordering of society in line with divine law. After the crushing military defeat in the Peasants' War, communalism lost much of its momentum, but remained a feature of the political landscape right through the early modern period.

Communalism has clearly informed much of the argumentation in this survey, particularly the constitutional similarities between urban and rural contexts, the ideological emphasis on the 'common good' and the political relevance of the common people within and beyond their localities. At the same time, this book operates with different definitions and emphases: the attribute 'communal' is assigned to any local topographical unit with independent resources and responsibilities, placing less weight on its autonomous creation through a voluntary union (hence the inclusion of originally 'ecclesiastical' bodies like parishes), but more on the active acquisition of collective capacity and the difficult negotiation of internal differences. It is thus intended as a study of the complexity, potential and inherent tensions of 'communal culture' in general rather than of the concept of 'communalism' in the narrower sense.

Like other seminal oeuvres, Blickle's work has sparked lively debate, especially among Germanic and Anglophone scholars [cf. 281: 99–100]. Many praised its contribution to history 'from below' and the interweaving of political and religious approaches – one reviewer classed *The Communal Reformation* as 'the most important work in the social history of the Reformation' for a generation [65a]. The most significant endorsement to date derives from Michael Mitterauer, who acknowledged communalism – alongside a closely interrelated bundle of other phenomena – as a 'particularly significant and influential factor' setting Europe on its distinctive trajectory from the medieval period. Identifying common origins, shared structures and similar political roles of urban and rural communes enables comparative historians to broaden Max Weber's emphasis on the 'autonomous town' into a socially much more comprehensive peculiarity of the West. The fact that some villagers and burghers acquired formal political rights in representative assemblies and others managed to link their localities into sovereign confederations appears equally unique in global perspective [257: 287; for a transatlantic instrumentalization of the concept see 298].

On the other hand, communalism has attracted criticism on a number of grounds. Concerns about the concentration on southwestern Germany and a lack of engagement with gender relations have already been touched upon. As a self-declared 'individualist', i.e. a historian inclined to stress the autonomy of peasant production and the economic causes of rural revolts, rather than a 'communalist', who affirms the importance of collective bonds and the political core of peasant risings, Tom Scott has been particularly vociferous, challenging Blickle's ideas of strong links between towns and villages on the one hand and the alleged affinity between communal and Protestant principles on the other [e.g. 62: 388 and chapters 6, 2; on the need to distinguish between quasi-'aristocratic' urban and 'democratic' rural communities see also 209: 214]. In the wake of the cultural turn, postmodern scholars of ceremony, ritual and discourse queried the strong focus on socio-political structures, charging Blickle with a romanticized view of a locally-based Old Europe and a disregard for the multi-dimensional complexity of historical developments [304]. Articulating the perhaps most persistent concern, Bob Scribner questioned the coherence and egalitarian character of the communes, pointing to the exclusion of major sections of inhabitants and the concentration of real power in the hands of narrow magisterial elites. For him and others, the harmonious character of communalism smacked of a desire to provide Germany – so often linked to authoritarian traditions – with a more presentable, 'democratic' past [63; cf. 130]. Within Switzerland, too, there has been a tendency to relativize the significance of the communal element in the origin and evolution of the Confederation; many historians now emphasize political opportunism rather than collectivist ideology, the leadership of social elites – including nobles – rather than peasant initiative and the need to take greater account of external forces and subject territories rather than to restrict discussion to the major cantons [see e.g. 268 and most recently 306].

Many of these points help to refine and adapt our understanding of local society and some – like the compatibility of communal principles with different confessions; the ambivalence between inclusion and exclusion; closer attention to gender roles and communication structures – are reflected in the chapters above. Yet communalism has been instrumental in transforming our views of the pre-modern world and aspects like similarities between town and village organization, interactions between the secular and spiritual spheres and the historical significance of political agency 'from below' are likely to stand the test of time. The fact that a cluster of autonomous rural communities managed to forge a lasting alliance with neighbouring cities, furthermore, suggests that revisionism on the Swiss Confederation should not be carried too far.

Communalism has also helped to revitalize debates on republicanism after decades of preoccupation with 'absolutist' regimes. For Blickle, towns and villages had an inbuilt preference for representative rather than monarchical forms of government; an idea taken up by Wolfgang Reinhard: 'The more advanced the development of communalism, the stronger the latent republicanism, the more likely the emergence of a republic, ... whose members not only have the freedom of self-determination, but above all the freedom from external monarchical control' [264: 240]. In communal heartlands like the Grisons, where commoners managed to realize their political ideals to a very large extent, they devised an integrated pyramid of local councils, regional assemblies and territorial leagues. By the 1520s, political power was delegated upwards via elected officials; feudal lords – personified by the Bishop of Chur, intriguingly the same kind of ruler previously marginalized in the Italian cities – lost their dominant position; and communal values informed the conduct of public affairs.

In the northern Netherlands, a similarly decentralized, if much more urbanized, framework allowed the Dutch to rise to global pre-eminence in the seventeenth century. 'The desire to maintain local and regional "freedoms" [constituted] a major cause of the Revolt against Spanish authority, and the establishment of the Republic ... a triumph for this ... particularism' [261: 4]. Even though Holland became the most influential of the seven provinces, which formally obtained independence from Spain in 1648, the political structure provided plenty of room for autonomy at local and regional level. Surprisingly for most contemporary – and indeed modern – observers, this system proved very efficient. There was a quasi-princely figurehead from the House of Orange, but effective power rested in representative institutions ranging from city councils and provincial assemblies to the federal 'States-General'. The latter were dominated by mercantile elites of non-noble status, who provided their polity with a framework conducive to the growth of trade and industry. Alongside, the bulk import of grain from the Baltic allowed peasants to become agricultural entrepreneurs, specializing in 'market gardening' and the provision of high-value fruit, vegetables and even flowers for discerning urban consumers. On these foundations, the country went on to experience unprecedented economic prosperity; members of the middling sort evolved distinctive forms of self-representation – most notably in visual genres like the still life, domestic interiors or landscape scenes during the so-called 'Golden Age'; adherents of other faiths – the official religion was Calvinist – enjoyed a degree of informal toleration; while military and technological ingenuity propelled the Republic to the status of a European and colonial super-power. Given the small size of its home base and population, however, this position proved difficult to sustain, and signs of overstretch became apparent by 1700.

Where circumstances proved less favourable, as in the German lands or in France, urban – and more rarely rural – communes could hope for political representation in provincial, territorial and imperial assemblies (*Landtage*; *états provinciaux*) – as Mitterauer emphasizes, in itself a remarkable phenomenon; no fewer than sixty cities had the right to attend the diet of the Holy Roman Empire, and in Sweden even the peasantry obtained an institutional voice in the *Riksdag.* The English House of Commons – composed of a mixture of elected county gentlemen and urban representatives – dramatically enhanced its position over the course of the seventeenth century. While the respective states retained monarchical constitutions, republican visions could emerge in moments of crisis, as during the Spanish Comuneros rising in 1520, the peasants' war in the Archbishopric of Salzburg half a decade later, or in the radical proposals put forward by the English Levellers in the late 1640s. Calls for decentralization went too far even for regicide Oliver Cromwell, who feared that they would turn the realm into another Swiss Confederation [43: 20–23; 54: 128].

Back in 1996, Antony Black rightly regretted that 'historians of the commune and of republicanism seem unaware of each other' [Black in 212: 111]. The latter had focused above all on intellectual discourse and the tradition/evolution of key ideas in selected contexts. The first related to Ancient Greece and Rome, where city republics first flourished in places like Athens, Sparta or Rome and philosophers like Plato and Aristotle identified monarchy, aristocracy and democracy as the three main types of government. A second centred on the re-discovery and intense discussion of classical thought during the Italian Renaissance, most notably the evaluation of the respective merits of principalities and republics in the works of Niccolò Machiavelli and other Florentine writers. The third featured the contested political debates conducted in the 'prerevolutionary Atlantic', starting with the constitutional struggles of Stuart England, where conservative and radical voices assessed the specific benefits of a range of different regimes (and the monarchy was temporarily replaced by a commonwealth in the 1650s), and finally the Enlightened eighteenth-century ideas which inspired the American and French revolutions and the dawn of the modern period [222; 92: 54].

In the meantime, the situation has evolved significantly. Moving beyond this established canon of theorists, lawyers, canonists and political thinkers, recent research on republics has paid increasing attention to comparable traditions in other European regions, including Poland–Lithuania (where nobles held the reins of power) and urban communities in different parts of the Holy Roman Empire [216; Schilling in 219]. Republics north of the

Alps, after all, formed integral parts of the emerging state system following the Peace of Westphalia, which granted international recognition not just to the Dutch, but also the Swiss Confederation in 1648. While egalitarian in principle, neither proved immune to the general trends of oligarchization and power concentration. A select circle of patrician and merchant elites tended to monopolize access to the ruling bodies [218]. Yet communal values were not a spent force: a study of conflict in Swabian Imperial Free Cities at the end of the early modern period underlines that burghers still saw the council as a representative rather than sovereign institution. Tensions erupted around the annual oath swearing ceremony and townspeople resorted to higher courts as well as ritual forms of resistance to defend their constitutional principles, often with considerable success [83]. There has even been a reassessment of the extent and significance of civic participation in powerful monarchical polities like England, not just with reference to the constitutional debates and ruptures during the seventeenth century, but also for late medieval and Tudor times [214; 115; 221a]. Even so, 'mainstream' scholarly priorities continue to favour political thought over everyday practice, elite civil society over lowly parish assemblies and urban over rural environments. There are no references to parishes, villages or communalism, for example, in an otherwise exemplary collection on republicanism as a 'shared European heritage' [221b; 227].

Where these environments come into view, there is a tendency to downplay the significance of traditional towns, villages and parishes for the development of early modern republican consciousness on the one hand, and liberal notions of 'individual' political rights on the other [103: 59; 255]. According to Thomas Maissen's investigation of Swiss and Dutch political discourse, sustained reflection on 'republican' identities – with reference to Roman traditions, classical terminology and distinct forms of self-representation – only emerged in the seventeenth century. The rationale derived from the need for these rulers to legitimize their 'unusual' polities vis-à-vis the powerful princes who dominated the diplomatic stage at the time. Monarchs like Louis XIV looked down on the petty merchants and parvenus they had to interact with, hence the latter were at pains to insist that their regimes rested on the civic virtues of the select few. In other words, they portrayed themselves as states governed by quasi-noble elites rather than the disorderly multitude; as descendants of antique ideals rather than of medieval local communities [220]. In eighteenth-century Bern, both ruling patricians and foreign observers liked to draw parallels with ancient Rome, pointing, for instance, to public institutions like granaries, hospitals, state-of-the art roads, use of the SPQB ('Senatus Populusque Bernensis') inscription on official buildings and the republican state education provided in the *Äusserer Stand*, a kind of shadow parliament serving as a training ground for the offspring of the city elite [Kapossy in 227: 231–6].

From this point of view, the discourses and iconographies of enlightened republics seem far removed from the communal traditions of popular assemblies and 'common good' principles. As outlined in Part I, towns, villages and parishes emerged out of specific social, economic and religious circumstances after the first millennium. When rural communities like Gersau reflected on their autonomous form of government, they emphasized the visionary initiatives of their forefathers, the acquisition of specific liberties, the careful stewardship of generations of councillors and, above all, divine favour rather than classical models or theoretical insights by conciliarists, Macchiavelli, Jean Bodin or James Harrington [30; 210; 231]. Still, here as in other local communities, the long-term continuity of – and pride in – participatory traditions emerges very clearly from closer scrutiny of minute books, accounts and chronicles as well as the interactions with the outside world. To deny this cultural framework of civic involvement any role in the growth of republican awareness and the political legitimization of non-monarchical regimes does not seem very convincing. The absence of the technical term 'republic' in local written tradition until the late seventeenth century does not mean that none of its defining components were present.

In his case study of the emergence of direct democracy in the Swiss canton of Schwyz, to move to the period watershed around 1800, Benjamin Adler draws a similarly sharp distinction between the acquired, corporate liberties of pre-modern burghers on the one hand, and the universal human rights postulated by the French Revolution on the other. The latter were not welcomed by the old communal assemblies of Schwyz, because they eroded their member's prerogatives, allocated all adult males an equal share in decision-making and accompanied moves towards centralization and bureaucratization. 'Communalism' thus appears as an outdated model, which enabled some members of the third estate to treat others in dependent territories as subjects. 'Liberty ... understood as a privilege, was – in exact opposition to the idea of human rights – based on inequality' [209: 207]. There was also no 'modern' division of power between the executive, legislative and jurisdictional spheres.

With the benefit of historical hindsight, such judgements can certainly be made, even though many liberal regimes belied their human rights rhetoric by opting for restrictive, property-based franchises (*Zensuswahlrecht*) themselves. Compared to the feudal regimes which predominated up to the late eighteenth century, in any case, the old burghers of Schwyz considered their system entirely 'democratic' and they proved able to adapt the governing *Landsgemeinde* to new circumstances, for instance through the integration of previously excluded sections of the population. To speak solely of ruptures and French imports would thus be misleading as well. Here, as in other communal heartlands, direct democracy was perceived as an extension of *ancien régime* participation, in the sense that the latter had prepared the ground through congenial cultural traditions and centuries of popular political involvement [Andreas Suter in 209: 223, 262]. The exact combination of tradition and innovation varied from place to place, but there can be no doubt that the old communal systems represented *relatively* – albeit never fully – representative forms of socio-political organization. The evolution of modern democracies drew on a wide range of intellectual and contextual influences, which included communal-republican precedents as well as liberal political thought and revolutionary advances [211]. As has been argued for the Commonwealth of Poland–Lithuania, where the early modern 'accumulation of powers by the citizenry' was also unusually extensive, traditions of representation 'were neither guarantors of modern notions of liberty, nor could they be embedded into a smooth teleological narrative of the birth of democracy, but they relied on "consensus systems", able to create a common *modus vivendi* for groups with very different confessional, regional and national identities' [216: xv].

Alongside communalism and republicanism, two further approaches should be considered. 'Microhistory' employs a reduction in scale to obtain a fuller understanding of the topic of investigation. Methods and terminology vary between different historiographical schools (from protagonists of Italian *microstoria* to sections of English local history), but by focusing on a single settlement or even individual, scholars have been able to extract very detailed information about the structures, processes and identities of pre-modern society. While the empirical evidence is inevitably patchy, techniques like record linkage have yielded remarkable reconstructions of everyday life in villages like Earls Colne and Terling in England or Neckarhausen in Germany. In response to questions about typicality and marginality, practitioners have argued that zooming in on the smallest units allows the dissection of macrohistorical processes – such as social polarization or proto-industrialization – as if under a microscope. It is fair to say, however, that most studies in the field have focused on socio-economic conditions, popular mentalities and interpersonal networks rather than communal structures as such [256; 157; 145].

'Communitarianism', finally, serves as a loose umbrella term for a body of recent critiques of Western liberalism, sometimes with explicit reference to societies of the past. Robert Putnam, for example, used Renaissance cities to underline the importance of collective institutions and civic engagement for good government, while Michael Taylor identified the principle of generalized reciprocity – according to which support of needy neighbours at particular points might be rewarded with help for oneself on other occasions – as a key feature allowing communities to flourish without state interference. A number of further issues, like the relationship between 'thick trust' – built up in daily interaction with families or patronage networks – and 'thin trust' – e.g. between citizens with lesser personal ties – have stimulated diachronic comparison, but the primary motivations for communitarians lie elsewhere. Given the perceived 'collapse' of modern social bonds through unrestrained self-interest, research is driven by current political and ideological concerns [223; 226; cf. 96: 4–6].

Summary

Members of local communities reflected their polities in differentiated ways and developed congenial forms of representation which catered for internal as well as external audiences. Emanating from specific socio-economic contexts, communal units interacted with the intellectual movements of the time, whose protagonists often derived inspiration from personal experience of town, village and parish life. Modern concepts like communalism and republicanism have helped to illuminate the structures and meanings of local association, even though scholarly dialogue across different fields and disciplines could be intensified further. There were no linear connections between *ancien régime* communities and modern direct democracy, but the cultural traditions and social depth of local government certainly informed the complex processes which produced the western European states we are familiar with today.

7 Conclusions

Twenty-first-century Europeans are used to go 'large': multinational companies, long-haul flights, steady EU expansion, global media empires and easy access to the World Wide Web form part of everyday experience. This book, in contrast, focuses on a period in which people tended to think 'small': more limited spatial horizons, closer embedding in kinship groups, humbler economic ambitions and, as highlighted here, stronger communal ties. Between *c.* 1100 and *c.* 1800, hundreds of thousands of towns, villages and parishes shaped the lives of literally billions of inhabitants – ironically enough, a phenomenon of truly 'massive' proportions.

Local communities, as defined in this book, had a close topographical focus. Rights and obligations derived from one's stake within a place of residence. Its exact boundaries, however, fluctuated according to context. Over and above expansion or contraction as a result of conquest, purchase or negotiation, contours varied depending on whether belonging was understood legally, economically or emotionally. Rather than grids imposed on an inert landscape, demarcations evolved situationally, a feature underlined by the periodic re-construction of community through processions, beating of the bounds and other forms of symbolic communication. The study of pre-modern towns, villages and parishes must thus move beyond the analysis of constitutional structures towards cultural history in the widest sense.

Case studies of the three main types of local communities in Italian-, German- and English-speaking Europe revealed similarities as well as differences. Size, internal organization and dates of emergence varied, but all allowed their full members – typically male householders – to conduct local affairs with at least a degree of self-determination and relatively broad levels of participation. The wider political significance resulted from collective rights of

118

regulation, administration, jurisdiction and resource allocation in the hands of 'middling' people outside the traditional elites of nobility and clergy. Cities may have been the most dynamic and potentially powerful bodies, villages the most socio-economically coherent, but parishes – which transcended the urban/rural boundary, the profane/sacred spheres and (in terms of their spiritual functions) gender divisions – represent the most universal and only truly *territorial* unit of local organization. Rights and obligations linked with secular and ecclesiastical communities interacted in complex patterns, providing members with complementary and sometimes conflicting identities. While often cutting across secular boundaries, parishes offered burghers and peasants opportunities to 'sacralize' their communal structures by means of corporate involvement in ecclesiastical affairs.

Communal culture reflected the increasing complexity of the environment in which it flourished. There is plentiful evidence for shared values, local pride and collective action, but it would be wrong to speak of uniformly harmonious relations or hermetic isolation. Burghers, peasants and parishioners – all socially heterogeneous groups in their own right – shaped communal affairs through (sometimes acrimonious) negotiation, in which power was unequally distributed and often concentrated in the hands of local elites. Internal factions and external forces also strove to affect decision making, while marginal groups and female inhabitants exercised informal influence, even though they lacked official enfranchisement. Cohesion and tensions were effectively two sides of the same coin.

Preceded by the predominance of *feudal* bonds between lords and tenants up to the High Middle Ages and succeeded by the rise of *individual* human rights and *national* affiliations in the wake of the liberal revolutions around 1800, the *Communal Age* constitutes a distinctive, more collective phase in Western European history. In many ways, its emphasis on the association of the *many* – significantly 'commoners' rather than 'aristocrats' – facilitated the transition from government by the *few* – nobles and prelates – towards that of *all* citizens – very gradually achieved in modern times and, for women, not until the twentieth century. While neighbourly ties existed before the first millennium and persist in the present, the greatest political, economic, religious and cultural significance of local communities coincided with the late medieval and early modern centuries. In this sense, they remind historians of long-term continuities across the traditional watershed around 1500, when the combination of technological, religious and cultural change suggests the dawn of a new era in other respects.

Yet the Communal Age included dynamic elements of its own. The centuries before 1500 witnessed the steady – and ultimately extensive – communalization of local society (usually coexisting with, but at times challenging the feudal order), those after brought processes of adaptation, in which towns, villages and parishes re-defined their role in the face of growing state and Church powers, religious fragmentation, educational differentiation and market exchange. Some retained near-total autonomy (defying contemporary claims that sovereignty needed to be centralized to create sustainable polities), others became mere enforcement tools of higher authorities, but most managed to give post-Reformation developments a distinctly local texture. The need to integrate ever more heterogeneous individuals tested local cohesion to its limits, but the communal framework survived. Urban oaths, village by-laws and parochial poor relief can still be found at the end of our period, although many collective ceremonial customs had indeed vanished. At the same time, in a transformation of communication structures, traditional face-to-face exchange was supplemented with growing recourse to script, print and long-distance interaction even in the most peripheral locations.

This investigation has surveyed extensive source materials and historiographical debates on a specific phenomenon in a closely circumscribed geographical context. It does not imply that communal organization was the *only* significant or transformative feature during these centuries, nor can it claim that the findings apply for Europe as a whole – even though there were hints of comparable developments in some eastern and Scandinavian areas. What the book does propose is that towns, villages and parishes empowered common people, by giving them opportunities to shape both *local* life – informed by remarkably 'advanced' principles like elections, accountability and the common good – and *central* polities – through instruments like petitioning, representation and ultimately rebellions. We should not exaggerate their emancipatory potential – the prevalent emphases on custom, religious conformity, moral supervision, corporate prerogatives and patriarchal rule mark fundamental differences compared to the modern western world – but each local community represented a social construct whose significance was greater than that of the sum of its parts. Towns, villages and parishes were fundamental building blocks of late medieval and early modern Europe.

Bibliography

I. Primary sources

Towns and cities

1. Carlotto, N. and Varanini, G. M. (eds), *Il "Regestum Possessionum Comunis Vincencie" del 1262* (Roma, 2006). An extensive list of the communal possessions of the Italian city of Vicenza during a period of autonomy.
2. Compagni, D., *Cronica delle cose occorrenti ne' tempi suoi*, ed. Gabriella Mezzanotte (Milan, 1993). A chronicle of political events in thirteenth-century Florence.
3. Freising, O. of [with co-author Rahewin], *The Deeds of Frederick Barbarossa*, trans. Charles C. Mierow and R. Emery (New York, 1953). This chronicle by the twelfth-century Bishop of Freising contains a contemporary perspective on Italian city communes.
4. Godding, P. and Pycke, J. (eds), 'La paix de Valenciennes de 1114: Commentaire et édition critique', in: *Bulletin de la Commission Royale pour la publication des anciennes lois et ordonnances de Belgique* 29 (1979), 1–142. One of the oldest surviving town charters for the Netherlands and northern France.
5. Kowaleski, M. (ed.), *Medieval Towns: A Reader* (Peterborough, Ontario, 2006). With selected documents/commentary on Italian city communes.
6. Michielin, A. (ed.), *Gli Acta Comunitatis Tarvisii del Sec. XIII* (Rome, 1998). Highlights the wealth of documentation surviving for thirteenth-century Treviso.
7. Schilling, D., *Die Luzerner Chronik des Diebold Schilling 1513: Eine wissenschaftlich bearbeitete Faksimile-Ausgabe* (Lucerne, 1977). Facsimile of an illustrated city chronicle presented to the council of Lucerne in 1513.

Villages and rural communities

8. Bailey, Mark (ed.), *The English Manor, c. 1200–1500: Selected Sources* (Manchester, 2002).

9. Bärtschi, A. (ed.), 'Die Chronik Josts von Brechershäusern', in: *Burgdorfer Jahrbuch* 25 (1958), 79–132. A record of local, regional and global events compiled by a prosperous Swiss peasant in the seventeenth century.

10. Blickle, P. and Holenstein, A. (eds), *Agrarverfassungsverträge: Eine Dokumentation zum Wandel in den Beziehungen zwischen Herrschaft und Bauer am Ende des Mittelalters* (Stuttgart, 1996). A collection of quasi-constitutional statements on the duties and obligations of tenants in a range of south German manors.

11. Dobson, R. B. (ed.), *The Peasants' Revolt of 1381* (London, 1970 [1983 edn]). A collection of sources relating to origins, stages and consequences of the great rural rising led by Wat Tyler and John Ball.

12. Gersau (Canton of Schwyz/Switzerland), District Archive [*Bezirksarchiv*]:
   —Books [*Bücher*], GST: Book of the Burgher Families of the Commune of Gersau (1627–1870); LB 4: Landbook no. 4 (1762)
   —Charters [*Urkunden*], no. 3: Alliance with the Forest Cantons (1359); no. 6: Purchase of feudal rights (3 June 1390); no. 8: Confirmation of liberties by the Emperor Sigismund (1433); no. 9: Legal code (1436); no. 10. Marriage law (1436); no. 12: Purchase of advowson (1483); no. 43: Conveyance of parish benefice (1726).

13. Grimm, J. (ed.), *Weisthümer* (7 vols, Göttingen, 1840–1878; reprint Hildesheim, 2000). Important nineteenth-century edition of German customary law.

14. *Österreichische Weistümer*, ed. Österreichische Akademie der Wissenschaften (Vienna, 1870–). Major series dedicated to editions of Austrian customary law.

15. Preis, C., *Bauernleben im Zeitalter des Dreissigjährigen Krieges. Die Stausebacher Chronik des Caspar Preis 1636–67*, ed. Wilhelm A. Eckhardt and Helmut Klingelhöfer (Marburg, 1998). Chronicle of the Hessian village of Strausebach during the Thirty Years War.

16. Scott, T. and Scribner, R. W. (eds), *The German Peasants' War: A History in Documents* (Atlantic Highlands, 1991).

17. Turner, T., *The Diary of Thomas Turner 1754–1765*, ed. David Vaisey (Oxford, 1984). These excerpts from a rural diary illuminate the life of a small shopkeeper and parish official.

Parishes

18. 'Audit Book of the Parish of Great St Mary's, Cambridge': Cambridgeshire County Record Office, P30/4/2.

19. Barnwell, P.S., Cross, C. and Rycraft, A. (eds), *Mass and Parish in Late Medieval England: The Use of York* (York, 2005). Text and translation of the medieval mass according to the use of York, with contextualizing essays and illustrations from a reconstruction.

20. Bishop Juxon's Survey of Parish Government and Fees in the Diocese of London (1636): Lambeth Palace Library, Carte Miscellanee, vol. ii, nos. 18, 72.
21. Borromeo, Carlo, 'Kardinal Borromeo, 30. September 1570', in: W. Oechsli (ed.), *Quellenbuch zur Schweizergeschichte* (2nd edn, Zurich, 1901), 461–9. Report on a journey through Central Switzerland by Cardinal [St] Carlo Borromeo in 1570.
22. Burgess, C. (ed.), *The Pre-Reformation Records of All Saints, Bristol* (3 parts, Bristol, 1995–2004). Edition of the uniquely rich and diverse archive of a metropolitan community, including accounts, wills, inventories, chantry records etc.
23. 'Churchwardens' Accounts of St Botolph Aldersgate, London': London, Guildhall Library/London Metropolitan Archives, MS 1454.
24. Dymond, D. and Paine, C. (eds), *The Spoil of Melford Church: The Reformation in a Suffolk Parish* (Ipswich, 1989 [rev. and extended edn, 2012]). Documents the impact of sixteenth-century change through a range of parochial and other records.
25. Hanham, A. (ed.), *The Churchwardens' Accounts of Ashburton 1479–1580* (Torquay, 1970). One of the fullest and most revealing sets of parish accounts, running right through the transformations of the Tudor period.
26. Klausner, D. N. (ed.), *Herefordshire and Worcestershire*, Records of Early English Drama (Toronto, 1990). Edition of evidence for early dramatic and mimetic activities, with much material from parish records.
27a. Lambert, Th. A. and Watt, I. M. (eds), *Registres du Consistoire de Genève au temps de Calvin*, vol. 1 : 1542–44 (Geneva, 1996). Edition of consistory court records from Geneva during the time of the Reformation.
27b. Lietzmann, H. (ed.), *Die Wittenberger und Leisniger Kastenordnung 1522/1523* (2nd edn, Berlin, 1935). Contains two early Lutheran parish ordinances.
28. Obermair, Hannes and Stamm, Volker (eds), *Zur Ökonomie einer ländlichen Pfarrgemeinde im Spätmittelalter. Das Rechnungsbuch der Marienpfarrkirche Gries (Bozen) von 1422 bis 1440* (Bozen/Bolzano, 2011). Edition (with commentary) of a rural set of churchwardens' accounts from South Tyrol.
29. Todd, Margo (ed.), *The Perth Kirk Session Books 1577–1590* (Scottish History Society, 2012). Illustrates and contextualizes the business of a Reformed consistory court, including presentations and punishments for offences like absences from church, adultery, drunkenness, fornication and slander.
30. Wiget, J., 'Die Turmkugel-Dokumente der Pfarrkirche Gersau', in: *Mitteilungen des Historischen Vereins des Kantons Schwyz* 76 (1984), 161–175. Edition of a series of parish chronicles written at Gersau (in present-day Switzerland) on the occasion of major church repairs and stored in a capsule on top of the spire.

31. Wood-Legh, K. L. (ed.), *Kentish Visitations of Archbishop Warham and his Deputies 1511–1512* (Kent Archaeological Society, 1984). Probably the most illuminating documentary survey of the issues and processes associated with ecclesiastical visitations.

Political thought

32. Althusius, J., *Politica methodice digesta et exemplis sacris et profanis illustrata* (Herborn, 1603). Outlines a multi-layered state organization based on the voluntary *consociatio* of local corporations into provinces.
33. Aristotle, *Politics*, trans. Ernest Barker (new ed., Oxford, 2009). A classic analysis of different forms of government from Greek Antiquity.
34. Haller, W. and Davies, G. (eds), *The Leveller Tracts 1647–53* (Gloucester, MA, 1964). Sources illustrating the demands of the Leveller movement in the English revolution.
35. Rousseau, J.-J., *Du contrat social, ou, Principes du droit politique* (Amsterdam, 1762). Devises a socio-political organization emerging from the free expression of the 'general will'.

Other source collections

36. Leadam, I. S. (ed.), *Select Cases in the Court of Requests 1497–1569* (London, 1898). Examples of proceedings before a Westminster equity court.
37. *Sammlung Schweizerischer Rechtsquellen*, ed. Schweizerischer Juristenverein (multiple vols, Aarau/Basel, 1898–). Canton-by-canton edition of legal records preserved in Swiss archives.

II. Secondary literature

General surveys and comparative studies

38. Armstrong, R. and Ó hAnnracháin, T. (eds), *Community in Early Modern Ireland* (Dublin, 2006).
39. Blickle, P., *Communal Reformation: The Quest for Salvation in Sixteenth-Century Germany*, trans. Thomas Dunlap (Boston, 1992).
40. Blickle, P., *From the Communal Reformation to the Revolution of the Common Man*, trans. B. Kümin (Leiden, 1998). A convenient English summary of many of Blickle's seminal contributions to community studies.
41. Blickle, P. (ed.), *Gemeinde und Staat im Alten Europa* (Munich, 1998). Essay collection examining various channels through which local communities affected state building in pre-modern Europe.

42. Blickle, P., *Kommunalismus: Skizzen einer gesellschaftlichen Organisations-form* (2 vols, Munich, 2000). The most detailed development of the concept of communalism in European perspective.

43. Blickle, P., 'Kommunalismus und Republikanismus revisited', in: F. Hitz, C. Rathgeb and M. Risi (eds), *Gemeinden und Verfassung: Bünd-ner Politik und Gebietsstruktur gestern, heute, morgen* (Chur, 2011), 13–34. A recent, concise summary of Blickle's concepts.

44. Burke, P., *Languages and Communities in Early Modern Europe* (Cambridge, 2004).

45. Calhoun, C. J., 'Community: Toward a variable conceptualization for comparative research', *Social History* 5 (1980), 105–29.

46. Cohen, Anthony P., *The Symbolic Construction of Community* (London, 1985).

47. Crow, G., *What are Community Studies?* (London, 2011). A guide for research on present-day communities.

48. Epstein, S. R. (ed.), *Town and Country in Europe 1300–1800* (Cambridge, 2001). A helpful, comparative essay collection.

49. Esposito, R., *Communitas: The Origin and Destiny of Community*, trans. T. Campbell (Stanford, 2010).

50. Gierke, O. von, *Das deutsche Genossenschaftsrecht* (4 vols, Berlin, 1868–1913) [selected passages in: *Community in Historical Perspective*, trans. M. Fischer, ed. A. Black (Cambridge, 1990)]. A classic text on the history of association.

51. Halvorson, M. J. and Spierling, K. E. (eds), *Defining Community in Early Modern Europe* (Aldershot, 2008).

52. Harrington, J. F. and Walser Smith, H., 'Confessionalization, com-munity and state building in Germany, 1555–1870', in *Journal of Modern History* 69 (1997), 77–101.

53. Hillery, G. A. Jr, 'Definitions of community: Areas of agreement', *Rural Sociology*, 20 (2/1955), 111–23.

54. Kümin, B., 'The fear of intrusion: Communal resilience in early modern England', in: W. Naphy and P. Roberts (eds), *Fear in Early Modern Society* (Manchester, 1997), 118–36.

55. Macfarlane, A., *Reconstructing Historical Communities* (Cambridge, 1977). Proposes a methodology to collect, relate and interpret differ-ent kinds of records relating to one locality.

56. Michaud-Quantin, P., *Universitas: Expressions du mouvement com-munautaire dans le Moyen-Age latin* (Paris, 1970). A legal study of corporations.

57. Molho, A., Curto, D. R. and Koniordos, N. (eds), *Finding Europe: Discourses on Margins, Communities, Images* (New York, 2007).

58. Parker, C. H. and Bentley, J. H. (eds), *Between the Middle Ages and Moder-nity: Individual and Community in the Early Modern World* (Lanham, MD, 2007).

59. Reynolds, S., *Kingdoms and Communities in Western Europe 900–1300* (Oxford, 1984). Surveys the high medieval evidence for various types of communities.

60. Rippmann, D., *Bauern und Städter: Stadt-Land Beziehungen im 15. Jahrhundert. Das Beispiel Basel* (Basel, 1990). Case study of late medieval city–country relations in the region around Basel.
61. Saulle Hippenmeyer, I., 'Gemeindereformation – Gemeindekonfessionalisierung in Graubünden. Ein Beitrag zur Forschungsdiskussion', in: H. R. Schmidt, A. Holenstein and A. Würgler (eds), *Gemeinde, Reformation und Widerstand. Festschrift für Peter Blickle zum 60. Geburtstag* (Tübingen, 1998), 261–80. Emphasizes the personal and contextual factors in local decisions for and against the Reformation.
62. Scott, T., *Town, Country and Regions in Reformation Germany* (Leiden, 2005). Reprints of important essays on peasant resistance, economic landscapes and town–country relations.
63. Scribner, R. W., 'Communities and the nature of power', in: *idem* (ed.), *Germany: A New Social and Economic History* (vol. 1, London, 1996), 291–325.
64. Shepard, A. and Withington, P. (eds), *Communities in Early Modern England* (Manchester, 2000).
65a. Theibault, J., 'Review of *The Communal Reformation*', in: *Central European History* 26 (1993), 117–18.
65b. Tönnies, F., *Gemeinschaft und Gesellschaft* (Leipzig 1887) [*Community and Society*, trans. Charles P. Loomis (New York, 1957)]. A seminal text on the historical evolution from 'community' to 'society'.
66. Weber, G. and Weber, R. (eds), *Zugänge zur Gemeinde: Soziologische, historische und sprachwissenschaftliche Beiträge* (Cologne, 2000). An interdisciplinary essay collection on approaches to local communities.

Towns and cities

67. Aaslestad, K., *Place and Politics: Local Identity, Civic Culture, and German Nationalism in North Germany during the Revolutionary Era* (Leiden: Brill, 2005). Focuses on transformations in the city of Hamburg around 1800.
68a. Altorfer-Ong, S., *Staatsbildung ohne Steuern: Politische Ökonomie und Staatsfinanzen im Bern des 18. Jahrhunderts* (Baden, 2010). German version of 'State-Building without Taxation: The Political Economy of State Finance in the Eighteenth-Century Republic of Bern' (PhD London School of Economics, 2007).
68b. Amelang, J. S., 'People of the Ribera: Popular politics and neighbourhood identity in early modern Barcelona', in: B. B. Diefendorf and Carla Hesse (eds), *Culture and Identity in Early Modern Europe 1500–1800* (Ann Arbor, 1993), 119–38.
69. Berengo, M., *L'Europa delle città: Il volto della società urbana europeo tra medioevo e età moderna* (Torino, 1999). A prominent survey work on European towns.

70. Bordone, Renato and Jarnut, Jörg (eds), *L'evoluzione delle citta italiane nell' XI secolo* (Bologna, 1988). Collection of essays on the evolution of Italian cities in the eleventh century.

71. Boulton, J., *Neighbourhood and Society: A London Suburb in the Seventeenth Century* (Cambridge, 1987). A pioneering survey of a communal sub-unit, with much quantitative analysis of demographic structures and migration patterns.

72. Brady, T. Jr, *Turning Swiss: Cities and Empire 1450–1550* (Cambridge, 1985). On the appeal of the Swiss Confederation for south German cities.

73a. Calabi, D., *The Market and the City. Square, Street and Architecture in Early Modern Europe* (Aldershot, 2003). Traces the key role of merchants in shaping medieval urban space and the transformations brought about by increasing regulation in the early modern period.

73b. Caminiti, G., *La vicinia di S. Pancrazio a Bergamo: Un microcosmo di vita politico-sociale (1283–1318)* (Bergamo, 1999). A case study of a medieval neighbourhood or ward in the Italian city of Bergamo.

74. Chittolini, G., 'Gli stati cittadini italiani', in: R. C. Schwinges et al. (eds), *Europa im späten Mittelalter: Politik – Gesellschaft – Kultur* (Munich, 2006), 153–65. Essay on Italian city states in the late medieval period.

75. Chojnacki, S., *Women and Men in Renaissance Venice: Twelve Essays on Patrician Society* (Baltimore, 2000).

76. Close, C. W., *The Negotiated Reformation: Imperial Cities and the Politics of Urban Reform 1525–50* (Cambridge, 2009). Stresses the role of urban networks in the spread of religious reform.

77. Coleman, E., 'The Italian communes: Recent work and current trends', *Journal of Medieval History* 25 (1999), 373–97.

78. Corteguera, L. R., *For the Common Good: Popular Politics in Barcelona, 1580–1640* (Ithaca, 2002). Focuses above all on the agency of artisans.

79. De Vivo, Filippo, *Information & Communication in Venice: Rethinking Early Modern Politics* (Oxford, 2007). A broad survey of communication structures in an early modern republic.

80. Dilcher, Gerhard, *Die Entstehung der lombardischen Stadtkommune: Eine rechtsgeschichtliche Untersuchung* (Aalen, 1967). A classic legal study of the emergence of communes in Lombardy.

81. Friedrichs, C. R., *The Early Modern City 1450–1750* (London, 1995). A useful textbook on early modern urban society.

82a. Garrioch, D., *Neighbourhood, Community and Sociability in Paris in the Second Half of the Eighteenth Century* (Oxford, 1983). Stresses the continuing strength of neighbourhood loyalties, forged by family, work and leisure activities.

82b. Gräf, H.T. and Keller, K. (eds), *Städtelandschaft – Réseau Urbain – Urban Network. Städte im regionalen Kontext in Spätmittelalter und Früher Neuzeit* (Cologne, 2004). Examines towns in their regional contexts during the late medieval and early modern periods.

83. Hafner, U., *Republik im Konflikt: Schwäbische Reichsstädte und bürgerliche Politik in der frühen Neuzeit* (Tübingen, 2001). Studies conflicts within South German imperial free cities towards the end of the early modern period.
84. Hansen, M. H. (ed.), *A Comparative Study of Thirty City-States Cultures* (Copenhagen, 2000).
85. Höh, M. von der, *Erinnerungskultur und frühe Kommune: Formen und Funktionen des Umgangs mit Vergangenheit im hochmittelalterlichen Pisa (1050–1150)* (Berlin, 2006). An interdisciplinary analysis of the various strands of communal memory in the high medieval city of Pisa, looking at written as well as architectural and artistic media.
86. Isenmann, E., *Die deutsche Stadt im Spätmittelalter: Stadtgestalt, Recht, Stadtregiment, Kirche, Gesellschaft, Wirtschaft* (Stuttgart, 1988). A comprehensive synthesis of the social, economic, religious and political life in late medieval German towns.
87. Jones, P., *The Italian City-State: From Commune to Signoria* (Oxford, 1997). A key survey of the Italian communal age.
88. Keller, H., *Adelsherrschaft und städtische Gesellschaft in Oberitalien (9.–12. Jahrhundert)* (Tübingen, 1979). Studies the relationship between feudal and urban society in Italy during the High Middle Ages.
89. Landwehr, A., *Die Erschaffung Venedigs: Raum, Bevölkerung, Mythos 1570–1750* (Paderborn, 2007). Emphasizes the active construction of a polity like 'Venice' during the period of early modern state formation by means of clearer definition of boundaries, use of censuses and the instrumentalization of myths.
90. Law, J. E. and Paton, B. (eds), *Communes and Despots in Medieval and Renaissance Italy* (Farnham, 2010). Collection of essays reassessing the broad spectrum of republican and despotic regimes in Italian city-states.
91. Lopez, R. S., *The Commercial Revolution of the Middle Ages 950–1350* (Cambridge, 1976).
92. Mackenney, R., *The City State 1500–1700: Republican Liberty in an Age of Princely Power* (Basingstoke, 1989).
93. Martines, L., *Power and Imagination: City-States in Renaissance Italy* (London, 1979).
94. Moeller, B., *Imperial Cities and the Reformation* (Philadelphia, 1972). Contains three essays on research problems, Humanism and Reformation change.
95. Muir, E., *Civic Ritual in Renaissance Venice* (Princeton, 1981).
96. Muir, E., 'The idea of Community in Renaissance Italy,' in: *Renaissance Quarterly* 55 (2002), 1–18.
97. Nevola, F., 'Introduction: Locating communities in the early modern Italian city', in: *Urban History* 37 (3/2010), 349–59.
98. Nicholas, D., *The Later Medieval City 1300–1500* (London, 1997).
99. Pfaff, C. (ed.), *Die Welt der Schweizer Bilderchroniken* (Schwyz, 1991). An introduction to the genre of illustrated city chronicles in the Swiss Confederation.
100. Pounds, N.J.G., *The Medieval City* (Westport, 2005).

Bibliography

101. Rau, S., *Geschichte und Konfession: Städtische Geschichtsschreibung und Erinnerungskultur im Zeitalter der Reformation und Konfessionalisierung in Bremen, Breslau, Hamburg und Köln* (Hamburg, 2002). A comparative study of the role of urban history-writing in northern German towns during the confessional age.

102. Rollison, D., *Commune, Country and Commonwealth: The People of Cirencester, 1117–1643* (Woodbridge, 2011).

103. Schlögl, R. (ed.), *Interaktion und Herrschaft: Die Politik der frühneuzeitlichen Stadt* (Constance, 2004). Essay collection on politics and communication in early modern towns.

104. Schlögl, R. (ed.), *Urban Elections and Decision-Making in Early Modern Europe, 1500–1800* (Cambridge, 2009). Essay collection examining the respective procedures and rituals in a range of case studies.

105. Scott, T., *The City-State in Europe, 1000–1600* (Oxford, 2012). A comparative approach focusing on the cities' territorial expansion and their lasting significance well beyond medieval Italy.

106. Settia, Aldo A. 'Pavia nell'età precomunale', in: *Storia di Pavia*, vol. 3/1 (Milan, 1992), 9–26. Traces the pre-history of the Italian commune of Pavia.

107. Skinner, Q., *Visions of Politics* (vol. 2, Cambridge, 2002). Collection of essays by the Cambridge intellectual historian.

108. Sutter, P., *Von guten und bösen Nachbarn: Nachbarschaft als Beziehungsform im spätmittelalterlichen Zürich* (Zurich, 2002). A good case study of the complex mixture of ties and tensions in urban neighbourhoods, exemplified for the late medieval Swiss city of Zurich.

109. Sweet, R., *The Writing of Urban Histories in Eighteenth-Century England* (Oxford, 1997).

110. Tittler, R., *Architecture and Power: The Town Hall and the English Urban Community* c. *1500–1640* (Oxford, 1991).

111. Trexler, R. C., *Public Life in Renaissance Florence* (Ithaca, 1991).

112. Violante, Cinzio, *La società milanese nell'età precomunale* (Bari, 1953). In-depth examination of Milanese society in the pre-communal age.

113. Waley, D., *The Italian City-Republics* (3rd edn, London, 1988). A clear and concise survey.

114. Walker, M., *German Home Towns: Community, State and General Estate 1648–1871* (new edn, Ithaca, 1998). A survey of the participatory culture in guild-based small towns on the eve of modernity, first published in 1971.

115. Withington, P., *The Politics of Commonwealth: Citizens and Freemen in Early Modern England* (Cambridge, 2005).

Villages and rural communities

116. Ault, W. O., 'Village assemblies in medieval England', in: *Album Helen Cam* (Louvain, 1960), 13–35.

117. Ault, W. O., 'Manor court and parish church in fifteenth-century England: A study of village by-laws', in: *Speculum* 42 (1967), 53–67.

118. Bader, K. S., *Studien zur Rechtsgeschichte des mittelalterlichen Dorfes* (3 vols, 1957–73). Influential survey on the legal history of medieval German villages.

119. Bierbrauer, P., 'Der Aufstieg der Gemeinde und die Entfeudalisierung der Gesellschaft im späten Mittelalter', in: P. Blickle and J. Kunisch (eds), *Kommunalisierung und Christianisierung: Voraussetzungen und Folgen der Reformation 1400–1600* (Berlin, 1989), 29–55. A summary of the development of rural communities in the late Middle Ages.

120. Blickle, P., 'Communal Reformation and peasant piety: The peasant Reformation and its late medieval origins', in: *Central European History* 20 (1987), 216–28.

121. Blum, J., 'The European village as community: Origins and functions', in: *Agricultural History* 45 (1971), 157–78.

122. Camenzind, J. M. M., *Die Geschichte von Gersau*, ed. Hans Georg Wirz (3 vols, Gersau, 1953–59). A history of the village republic of Gersau, with some source transcriptions, written by a local clergyman in the nineteenth century.

123. *Communautés rurales*, vol. IV: Europe occidentale (Paris, 1984). Essay collection on rural and parochial communities in pre-modern Europe.

124. De Moor, M., Shaw-Taylor, L. and Warde, P. (eds), *The Management of Common Land in North West Europe, c. 1500–1850* (Turnhout, 2002). Regional case studies assessing similarities and differences in the size, use and administration of common land.

125. Dyer, C., 'The English medieval village community and its decline', in: *Journal of British Studies* 33 (1994), 407–29.

126. Dyer, C. (ed.), *The Self-Contained Village? The Social History of Rural Communities 1250–1900* (Hatfield, 2007). Critical reviews of the traditional notion of isolated and self-sufficient village communities.

127. Fontaine, L., 'Königliche Macht und lokale Herrschaftspraxis in den Bergen der Dauphiné des 17. Jahrhunderts', in: S. Brakensiek and H. Wunder (eds), *Ergebene Diener ihrer Herren? Herrschaftsvermittlung im alten Europa* (Cologne, 2005), 185–202. Examines the changing relationship between royal power and local government in the French mountains of the Dauphiné.

128. Forster, M., *The Counter-Reformation in the Villages: Religion and Reform in the Bishopric of Speyer, 1560–1720* (Ithaca, 1992).

129. Fossier, R., *Peasant Life in the Medieval West*, trans. J. Vale (Oxford, 1988).

130. Friedeburg, R. von, '"Kommunalismus" und "Republikanismus" in der frühen Neuzeit? Überlegungen zur politischen Mobilisierung sozial differenzierter ländlicher Gemeinden unter agrar- und sozialhistorischem Blickwinkel', in: *Zeitschrift für historische Forschung* 21 (1994), 65–91. Emphasizes social stratification and tensions in early modern German villages.

131. Fuhrmann, R., *Kirche und Dorf: Religiöse Bedürnisse und kirchliche Stiftung auf dem Lande vor der Reformation* (Stuttgart, 1995). A study of religious initiatives, especially foundations of masses and clerical benefices, by German villages on the eve of the Reformation.

132. Genicot, L., *Rural Communities in the Medieval West* (Baltimore, 1990).

133. Gutton, J.-P., *La sociabilité villageoise dans l'ancienne France. Solidarités et voisinage du XVIe au XVIIIe s.* (Paris, 1998 [first edn 1978]). A study of rural sociability in early modern France.

134. Hagen, W., *Ordinary Prussians: Brandenburg Junkers and Villagers 1500–1840* (Cambridge, 2002).

135. Hewlett, C., *Rural Communities in Renaissance Tuscany. Religious Identities and Local Loyalties* (Turnhout, 2009).

136. Kümin, B. (ed.), *Landgemeinde und Kirche im Zeitalter der Konfessionen* (Zurich, 2004). Essay collection on the relationship between rural communities and the Church in the confessional age.

137. Luebke, D. M., *His Majesty's Rebels: Communities, Factions, and Rural Revolt in the Black Forest, 1725–1745* (Ithaca, 1997).

138. Magagna, V., *Communities of Grain: Rural Rebellion in Comparative Perspective* (Ithaca, 1991). An original transcultural approach to resistance.

139. Mayer, T., *Die Anfänge der Landgemeinde und ihr Wesen* (2nd edn, 2 vols, Sigmaringen, 1986). A pioneering essay collection on the origins of rural communities first published in 1964.

140. Moon, D., *The Russian Peasantry 1600–1930: The World the Peasants Made* (London, 1999).

141. Ogilvie, S. C., 'Communities and the "second serfdom" in early modern Bohemia', in: *Past & Present* 187 (2005), 69–119.

142. Ogilvie, S. C., 'Village community and village headman in early modern Bohemia', in: *Bohemia* 46 (2/2005), 402–47.

143. Rebel, H., *Peasant Classes: The Bureaucratisation of Property and Family Relations under Early Habsburg Administration 1511–1636* (Princeton, 1983).

144. Robisheaux, T., *Rural Society and the Search for Order in Early Modern Germany* (Cambridge, 1989).

145. Sabean, D., *Power in the Blood: Popular Culture and Village Discourse in Early Modern Germany* (Cambridge, 1984).

146. Schedensack, C., *Nachbarn im Konflikt. Zur Entstehung und Beilegung von Rechtsstreitigkeiten um Haus und Hof im frühneuzeitlichen Münster* (Münster, 2007). An examination of neighbourly disputes leading to civil litigation in an early modern German city.

147. Schnyder, Caroline, *Reformation und Demokratie im Wallis (1524–1613)* (Mainz, 2002). Case study of religious tensions and 'democratization' in the early modern Alpine republic of the Valais in present-day Switzerland.

148. Schulze, W., 'Peasant resistance in sixteenth- and seventeenth-century Germany in a European context', in Kaspar von Greyerz (ed.), *Religion, Politics, and Social Protest* (Boston, 1984), 61–98.

149. Smith, R. M., '"Modernization" and the corporate village community in England: Some sceptical reflections', in: A. Baker and D. Gregory (eds), *Explorations in Historical Geography* (Cambridge, 1984), 140–79. Challenges the notion of isolated medieval rural communities and their sudden integration into larger units.

150. Sreenivasan, G., *The Peasants of Ottobeuren 1487–1726: A Rural Society in Early Modern Europe* (Cambridge, 2004). Provides new insights on the early modern rural economy and land/capital markets.

151. Teuscher, S., *Erzähltes Recht: Lokale Herrschaft, Verschriftlichung und Traditionsbildung im Spätmittelalter* (Frankfurt, 2007). A reinterpretation of the compilation and significance of customary law.

152. Theibault, J., *German Villages in Crisis: Rural Life in Hesse-Kassel and the Thirty Years' War 1580–1720* (Atlantic Highlands, 1995).

153. Troßbach, W., *Soziale Bewegung und politische Erfahrung: Bäuerlicher Protest in hessischen Territorien 1648–1806* (Weingarten, 1987). This case study for Hesse underlines the significance of the Imperial Cameral Court for rural protest movements.

154. Troßbach, W. and Zimmermann, C., *Die Geschichte des Dorfs: Von den Anfängen im Frankenreich zur bundesdeutschen Gegenwart* (Stuttgart, 2006). An overview of German villages from the medieval origins to the present day.

155. Warde, P., 'Law, the "commune", and the distribution of resources in early modern German state formation', in: *Continuity and Change* 17 (2/2002), 183–211.

156. Wickham, C., *Community and Clientele in Twelfth-Century Tuscany: The Origins of the Rural Commune in the Plain of Lucca* (Oxford, 1998).

157. Wrightson, K. and Levine, D., *Poverty and Piety in an English Village: Terling, 1525–1700* (2nd edn, Oxford, 1995). A classic study of social polarization in the wake of the Protestant Reformation.

158. Wunder, H., *Die bäuerliche Gemeinde in Deutschland* (Göttingen, 1986). Survey on the German village community.

Parishes and ecclesiastical communities

159. Becker, Judith, *Gemeindeordnung und Kirchenzucht. Johannes a Lascos Kirchenordnung für London (1555) und die reformierte Konfessionsbildung* (Leiden, 2007). A comparative study of John a Lasco's ordinances for reformed congregations in Emden and London.

160. Beyerle, K., 'Die Pfarrverbände der Stadt Köln im Mittelalter und ihre Funktion im Dienst des weltlichen Rechts', in: *Jahresberichte der Görres Gesellschaft* (1929–30), 95–106. Studies the secular role of parishes in medieval Cologne.

161. Blair, J., 'Introduction: From minster to parish church', in his (ed.), *Minsters and Parish Churches: The Local Church in Transition 950–1200* (Oxford, 1988), 1–19. Concise account of the formation of the parish network.

162. Blickle, P., '"Pfarrkirchenbürger"?', in: C. Hesse et al. (eds), *Personen der Geschichte, Geschichte der Personen* (Basel, 2003), 153–64. Examines the links between south German cities and their rural parishioners.

163. Bünz, E., 'Pfarreien und Pfarrgemeinden im spätmittelalterlichen Deutschland', in M. Ferrari and B. Kümin (eds), *Identitätsbildung und Kulturtransfer im europäischen Niederkirchenwesen vor 1600* (Wolfenbüttel, forthcoming *c.* 2013). A synthesis of work on parish communities in late medieval Germany.

164. Burgess, C. and Kümin, B., 'Penitential bequests and parish regimes in late medieval England', in: *Journal of Ecclesiastical History* 44 (4/1993), 610–30.

165. Burgess, C. and Duffy, E. (eds), *The Parish in Late Medieval England* (Donington, 2006). Proceedings of the 2002 Harlaxton Symposium on the same theme.

166. Carlson, E. 'The origins, functions, and status of the office of churchwarden, with particular reference to the diocese of Ely', in: M. Spufford (Hg.), *The World of Rural Dissenters 1520–1725* (Cambridge, 1995), 164–207.

167. Craig, J., 'Co-operation and initiatives: Elizabethan churchwardens and the parish accounts of Mildenhall', in: *Social History* 18 (1993), 357–80.

168. Craig, J., 'Parish religion', in: S. Doran and N. Jones (eds), *The Elizabethan World* (London, 2010), Chapter 13.

169. Drew, C. E. S., *Early Parochial Organization: The Origins of the Office of Churchwarden* (London, 1954).

170. Duffy, E., *The Voices of Morebath: Reformation and Rebellion in an English Village* (New Haven, 2001). Microhistorical study of Reformation change.

171. Duffy, E., *The Stripping of the Altars: Traditional Religion in England c. 1400–c. 1580* (2nd edn, New Haven, 2005). Seminal 'revisionist' account of the vitality of late medieval religion and the impact of the English Reformation; first published in 1992.

172. Dyas, D. (ed.), *The English Parish Church through the Centuries* (York, 2010). An interactive CD-ROM with thematic contributions by numerous specialists as well as 3-D models, video introductions and supporting materials.

173. French, K. L., *The People of the Parish: Community Life in a Late Medieval English Diocese* (Philadelphia, 2001). Case study of the diocese of Bath & Wells.

174. French, K. L., *The Good Women of the Parish: Gender and Religion after the Black Death* (Philadelphia, 2008). The fullest account of the role of female parishioners in the late medieval period.

175. French, K., Gibbs, G. and Kümin, B. (eds), *The Parish in English Life 1400–1600* (Manchester, 1997). Anthology of different approaches to the English parish.

176. Graves, P., 'Social Space in the English Medieval Parish Church', in: *Economy and Society* 18 (1989), 297–322. A pioneering 'spatial' approach to parish experience.

177. Harvey, D., 'Territoriality, parochial development, and the place of "community" in later medieval Cornwall', in: *Journal of Historical Geography* 29 (2/2003), 151–65.

178. Hindle, S., 'Hierarchy and community in the Elizabethan parish: The Swallowfield articles of 1596', in: *Historical Journal* 42 (1999), 835–51. Analyzes independent political initiatives by the parish elite.

179. Hindle, S., *On the Parish? The Micro-Politics of Poor Relief in Rural England*, c. *1550–1750* (Oxford, 2004).

180. Hindle, S. and Kümin, B., 'The spatial dynamics of parish politics: topographies of tension in English communities, *c.*1350–1640', in: B. Kümin (ed.), *Political Space in Pre-industrial Europe* (Farnham, 2009), 151–73. Examines changing power relations from a spatial perspective.

181. Hutton, R., *The Rise and Fall of Merry England: The Ritual Year 1400–1700* (Oxford, 1994). Surveys the origins and fate of English ceremonial customs.

182. Kent, J., 'The centre and the localities: State formation and parish government in England c. 1640–1740', in: *Historical Journal* 38 (1995), 363–404.

183. Kruppa, N. and Zygner, L. (ed.), *Pfarreien im Mittelalter. Deutschland, Polen, Tschechien und Ungarn im Vergleich* (Göttingen, 2008). Contributions on medieval parish life in four Central European countries.

184. Kümin, B., *The Shaping of a Community: The Rise & Reformation of the English Parish* c. *1400–1560* (Aldershot, 1996). Examines the religious, social and political dimensions of parish life based on a quantitative analysis of churchwardens' accounts.

185. Kümin, B., 'Oral and written communication in the late medieval English parish', in: P. Oelze and R. Schlögl (eds), *Schrift und Druck. Medien des Entscheidens und der Macht im politischer Raum der europäischen Vormoderne* (Hannover, forthcoming c. 2013).

186. Mayes, D., *Communal Christianity: The Life and Loss of a Peasant Vision in Early Modern Germany* (Boston, 2004). Stresses the resilience of communal values.

187. McIntosh, M., 'Local responses to the poor in late medieval and Tudor England', in: *Continuity and Change* 3 (1988), 209–45.

188. McIntosh, M., *Poor Relief in England 1350–1600* (Cambridge, 2012). Long-term analysis of almsgiving, hospital / almshouse foundations and parish aid, emphasizing the gradual (and often bottom-up) evolution of the system.

189. Palmer, R. C., *Selling the Church. The English Parish in Law, Commerce, and Religion, 1350–1550* (Chapel Hill, 2002). Focuses on leases of parochial benefices.

190. Paravicini Bagliani, A. and Pasche, V. (eds), *La parrocchia nel medio evo: Economia, scambi, solidarietà* (Rome, 1995). Essay collection on medieval French and Italian parishes.

191. Pitman, J., 'Tradition and exclusion: Parochial office-holding in early modern England – A case study from North Norfolk, 1580–1640', in: *Rural History* 15 (2004), 27–45.

192. Pounds, N. J. G., *A History of the English Parish: The Culture of Religion from Augustine to Victoria* (Cambridge, 2000).

193. Range, M., 'Communal assertiveness and the importance of pastoral care: Flooding and parochial reorganization on the German North Sea coast in the seventeenth century', in: *German History* 30 (2012), 22–44.

194. Reitemeier, A., 'Kirchspiele und Viertel als "vertikale Einheiten" der Stadt des späten Mittelalters', *Blätter für deutsche Landesgeschichte*, 141/2 (2005–6), 603–40. An examination of parishes and wards as subunits of late medieval German towns.

195. Rodes, R. E. Jr, *Ecclesiastical Administration in Medieval England* (Notre Dame, 1977).

196. Roffey, S., *The Medieval Chantry Chapel: An Archaeology* (Woodbridge, 2007). Uses view-shed analysis to reconstruct contemporary experiences.

197. Schmidt, H. R., 'Ehezucht in Berner Sittengerichten 1580–1800', in: R. Po-chia Hsia and R. W. Scribner (eds), *Problems in the Historical Anthropology of Early Modern Europe* (Wiesbaden, 1997), 287–321. A survey of consistory records of the city republic of Bern, emphasizing the limits of social disciplining and the ways in which women could instrumentalize local jurisdiction.

198. Snell, K. D. M., *Parish and Belonging: Community, Identity and Welfare in England and Wales 1700–1950* (Cambridge, 2006).

199. Spaeth, D. A., *The Church in an Age of Danger: Parsons and Parishioners 1660–1740* (Cambridge, 2000).

200. Stefanovitch, P., *Prikhod i prikhodkoe dukhovenstvo v Rossii v XVI–XVII vekakh* [The Parish and the Parish Clergy in Russia in the 16th and 17th centuries] (Moscow, 2002). Contains an English summary on pp. 318–20.

201. Strauss, G., 'Success and failure in the German Reformation', in: *Past and Present* 67 (1975), 30–63. Triggered a debate on the grassroots impact of the Lutheran Reformation.

202. Swanson, R. N., *Church and Society in Late Medieval England* (Oxford, 1989).

203. Tomlinson, E. M., *A History of the Minories* (London, 1907). Studies an exceptionally autonomous London parish.

204. Verein für Dithmarscher Landeskunde e.V. (ed.), *Geschichte Dithmarschens* (2000). A survey work documenting the remarkable history of a (temporary) north German parish republic.

205. White, D. P., 'Elaborated Woodwork in Devon Churches', in *Regional Furniture* 24 (2010), 121–78. Examines the dynamic process of church embellishment through interactions between parishes, artisans and patrons.

206. Williamson M., 'Liturgical polyphony in the pre-reformation English parish church: A provisional list and commentary', in: *Royal Musical Association Research Chronicle* 38 (2005), 1–43.

207. Wright, S. (ed.), *Parish, Church and People: Local Studies in Lay Religion 1350–1750* (London, 1988). A pioneering essay collection on the English parish.

208. Wrightson, K., 'The Politics of the Parish in Early Modern England', in Paul Griffiths, Adam Fox and Steve Hindle (eds), *The Experience of Authority in Early Modern England* (London, 1996), 10–46.

Republicanism and political thought

209. Adler, Benjamin, *Die Entstehung der direkten Demokratie. Das Beispiel der Landsgemeinde Schwyz 1780–1866* (Zurich, 2006). A case study of the transition from communal structures in the Ancien Régime to direct democracy in the rural Swiss canton of Schwyz.
210. Black, A., *Guild and State: European Political Thought from the Twelfth Century to the Present* (New Brunswick, NJ, 2003).
211. Black, A., 'Communal Democracy and its History', in: *Political Studies* 45 (2002), 5–20.
212. Blickle, P. and Luckner-Müller, E. (eds), *Theorien kommunaler Ordnung in Europa* (Munich, 1996). Proceedings of a conference on theories of communal organization in theology, law and political thought, including minutes of the discussion.
213. Blickle, R., 'From subsistence to property: Traces of a fundamental change in early modern Bavaria', in: *Central European History* 25 (1992), 377–85. Traces the erosion of the traditional ideal of a right to 'livelihood' through the growing insistence on the absolute primacy of private property.
214. Collinson, P., *De Republica Angloroum or, History with the Politics put back* (Cambridge, 1990). Views Tudor England as a monarchical republic.
215. Friedeburg, R. von and Seidler, M. J., 'The Holy Roman Empire of the German Nation', in: H. A. Lloyd, G. Burgess and S. Hodson (eds), *European Political Thought 1450–1700* (New Haven, 2007), 102–72.
216. Friedrich, K. and Pendzich, B. M. (eds), *Citizenship and Identity in a Multinational Commonwealth: Poland–Lithuania in Context 1550–1772* (Leiden, 2009).
217. Head, R. C., *Early Modern Democracy in the Grisons: Social Order and Political Language in a Swiss Mountain Canton, 1470–1620* (Cambridge, 1995). A study of political discourse in an autonomous environment.
218. Holenstein, A., Maissen, T. and Prak, M. (eds), *The Republican Alternative: The Netherlands and Switzerland Compared* (Amsterdam, 2008).
219. Koenigsberger, Helmut G. (ed.), *Republiken und Republikanismus im Europa der Frühen Neuzeit* (Munich, 1988). Essay collection on early modern republicanism.
220. Maissen, Thomas, *Die Geburt der Republic: Staatsverständnis und Repräsentation in der frühneuzeitlichen Eidgenossenschaft* (Göttingen, 2006). Traces the origins and background of republican self-consciousness in early modern Switzerland.

221a. McDiarmid, J. F. (ed.), *The Monarchical Republic of Early Modern England: Essays in Response to Patrick Collinson* (Farnham, 2007). Scholarly evaluations of the theses advanced in 214.

221b. Mijnhardt, W. M., 'The limits of present-day historiography of republicanism', in: *De Achttiende Eeuw* 37 (2005), 75–89. Calls for greater attention to non-Atlantic traditions.

222. Pocock, J.G.A., *The Machiavellian Moment: Florentine Political Thought and the Atlantic Republican Tradition* (Princeton, 1973). Seminal study of the intellectual trajectories of republican thought.

223. Putnam, Robert, *Bowling Alone: The Collapse and Revival of American Community* (New York, 2000). A contemporary appeal to restore traditional bonds of family, neighbourliness and community.

224. Skinner, Q., *The Foundations of Modern Political Thought* (2 vols, Cambridge, 1978).

225. Swiss National Museum (ed.), *Switzerland in the Making through the 12th to the 14th Century* (Baden, 2011). Features survey articles on the origins and early development of the Swiss Confederation, with comparative glances at the wider Alpine and Central European context.

226. Taylor, Michael, *Community, Anarchy and Liberty* (Cambridge, 1982). Argues that communities can prosper without state interference.

227. Van Gelderen, M. and Skinner, Q. (eds), *Republicanism: A Shared European Heritage* (2 vols, Cambridge, 2002).

Other studies

228. Asch, R. and Freist, D. (eds), *Staatsbildung als kultureller Prozess. Strukturwandel und Legitimation von Herrschaft in der Frühen Neuzeit* (Cologne, 2005). Essay collection on state formation as a cultural process.

229. Bartlett, R., *The Making of Europe: Conquest, Colonization and Cultural Change 950–1350* (London, 1993).

230. Bell, D. A., *Communitarianism and its Critics* (Oxford, 1993).

231. Black, A., *Council and Commune: The Conciliar Movement and the Fifteenth-Century Heritage* (London, 1979).

232. Blickle, P., *Das Alte Europa: Vom Hochmittelalter bis zur Moderne* (Munich, 2008). A new interpretation of the building blocks of pre-modern Europe.

233. Blickle, P., *Unruhen in der ständischen Gesellschaft* (2nd edn, Munich, 2010). A comprehensive review of riots and rebellions in the Holy Roman Empire.

234. Blockmans, W. and Genet, J.-P. (eds), *The Origins of the Modern State in Europe* (7 vols, Oxford, 1995–2000). Results of a collaborative European Science Foundation project.

235. Blockmans, W., Holenstein, A. and Mathieu, J. (eds), *Empowering Interactions: Political Cultures and the Emergence of the State in Europe*

1300–1900 (Farnham, 2009). Examines state building 'from below'.

236. Brenner, N., 'The Limits to Scale? Methodological Reflections on Scalar Structuration', *Progress in Human Geography*, 25 (2001): 591–614.

237. Burckhardt, J., *The Civilization of the Renaissance in Italy*, trans. S. Middlemore (London, 1960). Originally published in 1860, it became the classic account of Italy's contribution to the rise of the individual and the modern world.

238. Burke, P., *What is Cultural History?* (2nd edn, Cambridge, 2008).

239. Capp, B., *When Gossips Meet: Women, Family and Neighbourhood in Early Modern England* (Oxford, 2003). Emphasizes female agency and informal powers in early modern communities.

240. Cohn, H. J., 'Anticlericalism in the German Peasants' War 1525', in: *Past and Present* 83 (1979), 3–31.

241. Coy, J. P., Marschke, B. and Sabean, D. W. (eds), *The Holy Roman Empire, Reconsidered* (New York, 2010). Essay collection highlighting approaches of the new political history, with a special emphasis on the study of rituals and ceremonies.

242. Dülmen, R. van, *Die Entdeckung des Individuums 1500–1800* (Frankfurt a.M., 1997). Charts the rise of the individual between the Renaissance and Enlightenment.

243. Friedrich, K., *The Other Prussia: Royal Prussia, Poland and Liberty 1569–1772* (Cambridge, 2000). With a strong focus on the role of towns.

244. Galpern, A., *The Religions of the People in Sixteenth-Century Champagne* (Cambridge, MA, 1976).

245a. Gordon, B., *The Swiss Reformation* (Manchester, 2002).

245b. Gotthard, A., *In der Ferne: Die Wahrnehmung des Raums in der Vormoderne* (Frankfurt, 2007). Surveys perceptions of space in premodern Europe.

246. Graves, M. A. R., *The Parliaments of Early Modern Europe* (Harlow, 2001).

247. Head, R., 'Knowing like a state: The transformation of political knowledge in Swiss archives 1450–1770', *Journal of Modern History* 75 (2003), 745–82. A comparative study of record-keeping and information accessibility in early modern republics.

248. Headley, J. M., Hillerbrand, H. J. and Paplas, A. J. (eds), *Confessionalization in Europe, 1555–1700: Essays in Honour and Memory of Bodo Nischan* (Aldershot, 2004). Reviews an important concept in German historiography.

249. Hilton, R. H., *The Decline of Serfdom in Medieval England* (London, 1969).

250. Jorio, M. (general ed.), *Historisches Lexikon der Schweiz* (Basel, 2002–). New encyclopaedia of Swiss history with some 36,000 entries in 13 volumes, published simultaneously in three languages.

251. Jucker, M., *Gesandte, Schreiber, Akten. Politische Kommunikation auf eidgenössischen Tagsatzungen im Spätmittelalter* (Zurich, 2004). Examines

the complex interaction of oral and written media in the political culture of the Swiss Diet during the late Middle Ages.

252. Kümin, B., *Drinking Matters: Public Houses and Social Exchange in Early Modern Central Europe* (Basingstoke, 2007). Highlights public houses as the principal communication hubs in early modern communities.

253. Kümin, B., Würgler, A., 'Petitions, Gravamina and the early modern state: local influence on central legislation in England and Germany (Hesse)', in: *Parliaments, Estates and Representation* 17 (1997), 39–60.

254. Kümin, B., 'Political Culture in the Holy Roman Empire [Review Essay]', in: *German History* 27 (2009), 131–44.

255. Luebke, D. M., 'Participatory politics', in: P. Wilson (ed.), *A Companion to Eighteenth-Century Europe* (Oxford, 2008), 479–94.

256. Macfarlane, Alan, *The Origins of English Individualism: The Family, Property, and Social Transition* (Cambridge, 1978).

257. Mitterauer, M., *Warum Europa? Mittelalterliche Grundlagen eines Sonderwegs* (Munich, 2003; American edn: Chicago, 2010). A reinterpretation of the medieval foundations for Europe's distinct historical trajectory.

258. Muir, E., *Ritual in Early Modern Europe* (Cambridge, 1997).

259. Oexle, O. G., 'Soziale Gruppen in der Ständegesellschaft: Lebensformen des Mittelalters und ihre historischen Wirkungen', in: *idem* and A. v. Hülsen-Esch (eds), *Die Repräsentation der Gruppen: Texte, Bilder, Objekte* (Göttingen, 1998), 9–44. Offers an introduction to the concept of 'social groups' (e.g. guilds and local communities) within the pre-modern estate system.

260. Ogilvie, S. C., *A Bitter Living: Women, Markets and Social Capital in Early Modern Germany* (Oxford, 2003). Finds much female activity outside the domestic sphere, but also restraining influences by communes and guilds.

261. Prak, M., *The Dutch Republic in the Seventeenth Century* (Cambridge, 2005).

262. Radeff, A., 'Food systems: Central–decentral networks', in: B. Kümin (ed.), *A Cultural History of Food in the Early Modern Age* (Oxford, 2011), 29–46. Emphasizes the role of small-scale, decentral trade in early modern Europe.

263. Raeff, M., *The Well-Ordered Police State: Social and institutional change through law in the Germanies and Russia, 1600–1800* (New Haven, 1983).

264. Reinhard, W., *Geschichte der Staatsgewalt. Eine vergleichende Verfassungsgeschichte Europas von den Anfängen bis zur Gegenwart* (Munich, 2000). A comparative examination of state power in Europe from the origins to the present day.

265. Roberts, M., *The Age of Liberty: Sweden 1719–1772* (Cambridge, 1986).

266. Roper, L., '"The Common Man", "the Common Good", "Common Women": Gender and Meaning in the German Reformation Commune', in: *Social History* 12 (1987), 1–21.

267. Rubin, Miri, 'Small groups: Identity and solidarity in the late Middle Ages', in: J. Kermode (ed.), *Enterprise and Individuals in Fifteenth-Century England* (Stroud, 1991), 132–50.

268. Sablonier, R., *Gründungszeit ohne Eidgenossen: Politik und Gesellschaft in der Innerschweiz um 1300* (Baden, 2008). A strongly revisionist interpretation of the origins and basic structures of the Swiss Confederation.

269. Schilling, H., 'Luther, Loyola, Calvin und die europäische Neuzeit', in: *Archive for Reformation History* 85 (1994), 5–31.

270. Schindler, N., *Rebellion, Community and Custom in Early Modern Germany*, trans. P. E. Selwyn (Cambridge, 2002). Essays from an anthropological perspective.

271. Schnitter, H., *Volk und Landesdefension* (Berlin, 1977). A survey of local and communal military defence systems in early modern Germany.

272. Scott, Tom, *Society and Economy in Germany, 1300–1600* (Basingstoke, 2002).

273. Tarbin, S. and Broomhall, S. (eds), *Women, Identities and Communities in Early Modern Europe* (Aldershot, 2008). Collection of case studies exploring the tensions between shared gender identity and individual differences in a variety of regional / chronological contexts.

274. Te Brake, W., *Shaping History: Ordinary People in European Politics 1500–1700* (Berkeley, 1998).

275. Thompson, E. P., 'The moral economy of the English crowd in the eighteenth century', in: *Past & Present* 50 (1971), 76–136. A classic study of popular protest.

276. Tlusty, B. Ann, *The Martial Ethic in Early Modern Germany: Civic Duty and the Right of Arms* (Basingstoke, 2011).

277. Ullmann, S., *Nachbarschaft und Konkurrenz. Juden und Christen in Dörfern der Markgrafschaft Burgau 1650–1750* (Göttingen, 1999). Case study of Christian–Jewish relations in a southern German county.

278. Walker, G. (ed.), *Writing Early Modern History* (London, 2005). Anthology of current approaches.

279. Weber, M., *Wirtschaft und Gesellschaft: Grundriss der verstehenden Soziologie*, ed. J. Winckelmann (5th edn, Tübingen, 1972). One of the most influential works of the German sociologist, first published posthumously in the 1920s.

280. Wiesner, M. E., *Women and Gender in Early Modern Europe* (Cambridge, 1993). A useful textbook survey.

281. Wilson, P. H., *From Reich to Revolution: German History 1558–1806* (Basingstoke, 2004).

282. Würgler, A., 'Which Switzerland? Contrasting Conceptions of the Early Modern Swiss Confederation in European Minds and Maps', in: B. Kümin (ed.), *Political Space in Pre-industrial Europe* (Farnham, 2009), 197–213.

283. Zmora, H., *State and Nobility in Early Modern Germany: The Knightly Feud in Franconia 1440–1567* (Cambridge, 1997). Rejects the notion of a crisis of the aristocracy in favour of a mutual dependency of nobles and princes.

III. Web resources

Primary evidence

284. Althusius, J., *The Politics* [*Politica methodice digesta*] (3rd edn, 1614), ed./trans. F.S. Carney, http://www.constitution.org/alth/alth.htm (accessed 23 November 2012). Outlines a multi-layered state organization based on the voluntary *consociatio* of local corporations into provinces.

285. Apian, Phillip, *Bairische Landtaflen* (woodcuts, Ingolstadt, 1568), http://www.bayerische-landesbibliothek-online.de/histkarten (accessed 23 November 2012). Early maps of the principality of Bavaria.

286. Bordone, R. (ed.), *La Società urbana nell'Italia comunale* (Turin, 1984), http://fermi.univr.it/rm/didattica/fonti/bordone/indice.htm (accessed 25/3/2011). A collection of documents in thematic arrangement.

287. Braun, Georg, *Civitates Orbis Terrarum* (Cologne, 1572), http://historic-cities.huji.ac.il/ (accessed 23 November 2012). Maps of sixteenth-century cities.

288. 'Bremen Online: Der Bürgereid': http://bremen.de/der-bremer-buerger-eid-926120 (accessed 23 November 2012). The burghers' oath of the German city of Bremen.

289. Goldstainer, Paul, 'Gmünder Chronik' (1549–50), ed. by K. Graf and digitized by T. Gloning, http://www.uni-giessen.de/gloning/tx/1550glds.htm (accessed 23 November 2012). Chronicle of the South German Imperial Free City of Schwäbisch-Gmünd.

290. 'Earls Colne, Essex: Records of an English Village 1375–1854': http://linux02.lib.cam.ac.uk/earlscolne// (accessed 23 November 2012).

291. 'Ewiger Bund der drei Waldstätte' (1291): http://www.verfassungen.de/ch/ruetli91.htm (accessed 23 November 2012). Text of the 'Eternal League' of the three Forest Cantons.

292. Marshall, A., 'Medieval Wall Painting in the English Parish Church' (2008): http://www.paintedchurch.org/index.htm (accessed 23 November 2012).

293. 'Medieval Sourcebook: Barbarossa and the Lombards', http://www.fordham.edu/Halsall/source/barbarossa-lombards.asp (accessed 23 November 2012).

294. Rousseau, J.-J., *The Social Contract or Principles of Political Rights* [Le Contract Social] (1762), ed./trans. G.D.H. Cole, http://www.constitution.org/jjr/socon.htm (accessed 23 November 2012).

295. 'Stadtarchiv Duderstadt': http://www.archive.geschichte.mpg.de/duderstadt/dud-d.htm. Digital versions of all documents preserved in this German town archive up to 1650.

296. 'Villanelle : Association de l'Histoire du Village', http://umb-www-01.u-strasbg.fr/villanelle/ (accessed 23 November 2012). Website featuring an extensive collection of documents and commentaries on French rural history.

Secondary works and online platforms

297. 'Community platform My-Parish': http://my-parish.org (accessed 29 November 2012). A website supporting exchange between parish historians.

298. Dillinger, J., 'Comparing Communities: Local Representation and Territorial States in Early Modern Europe and New England', in: *Bulletin of the German Historical Institute (Washington DC)* 27 (Fall 2000), http://www.ghi-dc.org/publications/ghipubs/bu/027/b27dillingerframe.html (accessed 23 November 2012).

299. Doyno, M., 'Urban Religious Life in the Italian Communes: The State of the Field', in: *History Compass* 9 (9/2011), 720–30, DOI: 10.1111/j.1478-0542.2011.00790.x (accessed 23 November 2012).

300. 'The Experience of Worship', http://www.experienceofworship.org.uk/ (accessed 23 November 2012). Platform for the dissemination of research findings on late medieval English cathedral/parish liturgy, including audio-visual documentation of in-situ enactments.

301. Fasoli, G. and Bocchi, F. (eds), *La città medievale italiana* (Florence, 1973), http://centri.univr.it/RM/didattica/strumenti/fasoli_bocchi/indice.htm (accessed 23 November 2012). A concise survey intended for teaching purposes.

302. 'Polo Museale Fiorentino', official website of Florentine architecture and heritage, http://www.polomuseale.firenze.it/ (accessed 23 November 2012).

303. Smith, M. K., 'Community', in: *The encyclopedia of informal education* (2001), http://www.infed.org/community/community.htm (accessed 23 November 2012).

304. Stollberg-Rilinger, B., 'Review of: Blickle, Peter, *Das Alte Europa*', *H-Soz-u-Kult, H-Net Reviews* (September 2008), http://www.h-net.org/reviews/showrev.php?id=22726 (accessed 23 November 2012).

305. Stollberg-Rilinger, B., 'Much Ado About Nothing? Rituals of Politics in Early Modern Europe and Today', in: *Bulletin of the German Historical Institute (Washington DC)* 48 (Spring 2011), http://www.ghi-dc.org/files/publications/bulletin/bu048/bu_48_009.pdf (accessed 23 November 2012).

306. Teuscher, S., 'Dieses groteske Wirgefühl', in: *Tages-Anzeiger* (1 November 2011), http://www.tagesanzeiger.ch/zuerich/Dieses-groteske-Wirgefuehl/story/27626307 (accessed 23 November 2012). A newspaper article calling for a fresh approach to Swiss history.

Index

Page numbers in *italics* indicate illustrations

officials, 13–14, 18–19, 30, 33,
37, 41, 44, 46, 48–50, 52, 57,
61–2, 64–5, 70–3, 75, 77, 79,
87–8, 90, 92, 100, 103; and *see*
churchwardens, mayors
oligarchy, 23, 34, 49, 72, 113
oral(ity), 75
order, 63, 76
overlaps, 79

Padua, 62
pagan *see* magic
palaces, *21*, 22, *91*
Palatinate, 36
Paris, 65
parish(es), 1, 6–7, 11, 33, 40–53,
50, 55–6, 59, 65–6, 78–9, 87, 90,
98, 104, 108, 113, 117–21
parish churches, *32*, 43, *50*, 75, 79,
80, *91*, 98–9
parishioners, 31, 40–52, 57, 69, 72,
78–9, 83, 86, 88, 97, 99, 119; and
see parish
Parker, Charles H., 6
Parliament *see* representative
assemblies
participation (political), 1, 17–19,
22–3, 33, 48, 57, 62, 71–2, 77,
114–15, 118
parties, 2
patriarchy, 28, 38, 57, 63–4, 121
patronage, 2, 20, 46, 62, 64, 116
Pavia, 13
peace, 13, 30, 57, 68, 70, 80, 102,
104, 107; of Constance, 14; of
Westphalia, 34, 113
peasants, 1, 25–39, 79, 84–5, 88,
92, 99, 105, 107, 110–11, 119;
and *see* agriculture; villages
Peasants' War, English, 70;
German, 36–7, 65, 71, 86, 92,
105, 108; Swiss, 103
people *see* common people, *popolo*
perceptions, 6, 16, 97–104, 116
periodicals *see* news(papers)
periphery, 46, 90
petitions, 35, 76, 92, 108, 120
philosophy, 7

piety, 27, *32*, 33, 45, 103–4
pilgrim(age), 41, 48
Pisa, 22, 99
Pistoia, 19
Plato, 112
Pocock, J.G.A.
podestà, 19–20, 22
Poland-Lithuania, 29, 85, 112, 115
police *see* good police; police state
see state
polis, 5, 75, 104
political parties *see* parties
political rights, 4
political thought, 5, 19, 104–7
politics, 18–20, 31–5, 42–4, 46,
71–2, 93, 110; and *see* parties
poor, 11, 26
poor relief, 3, 41, 48, *50*, 58,
88–90, 116, 120
popes, 5, 47
popolo, 13, 18–19, *21*, 22, 62
popular culture, 63, 68
population, 11, 17, 19, 26, 37–8,
57, 84–5
postmodern, 109
power, 1, 48, 58, 83, 93, 115
preaching, 48–9, 87–9, 103
Preis, Caspar, 102
prelates, 12–14, 16–18, 26, 44–5,
47, 56, 58, 81, 86, 89, 111, 119
prices, 28
priests *see* clergy
primary sources *see* sources
princes, 35, 38–9, 60, 79, 81, 90,
92, 100, 105, 111, 113; and *see*
monarchy
print(ing), 47, 73, 75–6, 120
privileges *see* liberties
processions, 20, *74*, 97, 118
profit, 12
property, 68
Protestant, 38, 47–8, 51, 87,
105, 109; and *see* specific
denominations
proto-industry, 26–7, 83, 116
public houses, 20, 27, 30, 63–4, 75
public sphere, 12, 63, 73
public works, 42

urban *see* towns
urbanization, 3, 26, 85
Uri, 80

Valais, 81, 89
Valenciennes, 72
values, 1, 6, 22, 57, 67–71, 76, 79,
   93, 100, 107, 111, 113, 119
Venice, 17, 20, 23, 57, 66, 73, *74*,
   75, 98
vestries, 44, 47, 48–9, 71, 75
Vicenza, 66
Victorian period, 51–2
Vienna, 36
villages, vills, 1–3, 6–7, 11, 25–39,
   48, 55–6, 61–3, 78–9, 85, 98,
   102–4, 109, 113, 117–21; village
   halls, *32*, 75; and *see* agriculture;
   peasants
violence, 30, 65
Visconti dynasty, 22
visitations, 37, 44, 47, 49, 86–7, 90
viticulture, 27

Volterra, 13, 22
voluntary, 78, 80

Walker, Mack, 6
wall *see* town walls
wards *see* neighbourhoods
wars, 23, 36–7; and *see* civil wars,
   military affairs, Peasants' War,
   Thirty Years' War
Warwick, *50*
weapons of the weak, 35, 92
Weber, Max, 40, 51, 109
Westphalia, 34; and *see* peace
Withington, Phil, 6
women, 28–9, 44–5, 63–4, 119
writing, 19, 30–1, 46–7, 73, 75–7,
   99, 120
Württemberg, 26, 29

Yatton, 44

Zurich, 65, 88
Zwingli(anism), 83, 87, 104

Printed in China